07-CEP-590

Through the Eyes of Faith

by John Powell, S.J.

D0972888

ThomasMore®
– An RCL Company –

Allen, Texas

COVER PHOTO
Comstock Inc.

ACKNOWLEDGEMENT

Father John Powell's "American Catholic" columns are used with permission from EXTENSION Magazine, 35 East Wacker Drive, Chicago, IL, copyright 1985–91

Copyright © 1992 by John Powell

All rights reserved. No part of this book shall be reproduced or transmitted in any form or by any means, electronic or mechanical, including photocopying, recording, or by any information or retrieval system, without written permission from Thomas More.

Send all inquiries to:
Thomas More
An RCL Company
200 East Bethany Drive
Allen, Texas 75002-3804

BOOKSTORES:
    Call Bookworld Companies 888-444-2524 or fax 941-753-9396
PARISHES AND SCHOOLS:
    Thomas More Publishing 800-822-6701 or fax 800-688-8356
INTERNATIONAL:
    Fax Thomas More Publishing 972-264-3719

Visit our website at www.rclweb.com

Printed in the United States of America

ISBN 0-88347-330-5

3 4 5 6 7   03 02 01 00 99

Contents

Introduction

This book is a collection of articles by Father John Powell. They were originally published in *EXTENSION* Magazine over a seven-year period, from 1985 to 1991.

Some of the materials, stories, and illustrations can be found in one or another of Father Powell's thirteen previously published books. However, much of the material and all of the writing is original.

John Powell is one of the more popular Christian authors in America. His thirteen books, of which more than twelve million copies are in circulation, have been translated into twelve foreign languages. He has recently made a video program based on his last book, *Happiness Is an Inside Job.*

John Powell's combination of education, varied life experiences, and sensitivity to the human condition have inspired his writing. The essays that follow range over many topics: faith and the virtues, attitudes, the Beatitudes, Church, worry, memories, habits, and so forth. These essays penetrate the daily human existence that most of us know. They seem to express for us our hopes, struggles, and ideals. John Powell puts into words what most of us have experienced.

John sees himself as one of those, stationed by God's will, at the marriage of psychology and theology. It is his conviction that we cannot be holy without being humanly whole, and we cannot be whole without striving for holiness. This theme runs like a thread through the pages that follow.

In 1967 John began teaching at Loyola University in Chicago. He currently teaches theology at that university. Of this teaching experience he says, "I very much love and appreciate the young people I teach. They keep me in touch with contemporary reality, and I think they give as much to me as I am able to give to them. And this is the way God gives gifts to all of us: through one another."

Finally, one of John Powell's deepest convictions is that the Gospel should be presented as "good news." The overview of faith is optimistic. God is love. We are loved by God, who is our origin and eventual destiny. Someday we will celebrate with God in God's house, and the celebration will be forever and ever. This is what John Powell believes. It is against this background of hopefulness that John Powell writes.

Tabor Publishing
Allen, Texas
1992

Faith: The God Connection

The French Emperor, Napoleon I, once asked his famous astronomer, Pierre Laplace, to make a diagram of all reality. When Laplace brought the finished drawing to the Emperor, Napoleon asked: "And where is God?" The scientist replied: "I have no need for such an hypothesis to explain the world."

God was not in Laplace's picture. I ask myself: To what extent is God in my picture? If I were to make a diagram of all reality, representing everything and everyone that is important to me by a larger or smaller circle, depending on importance and meaning, how large would my God-circle be?

In the end it is a matter of faith, isn't it? Faith alone puts God into the picture and the dimensions of my faith determine the size of my God-circle.

And what is faith? Whenever we make an act of faith, we take something as true on the word of another. All love relationships somehow begin with and are built on an act of faith. If you tell me that you love me, I cannot logically prove it or disprove it. I cannot ask you to do so. There is no final proof. Only your word. I can take your word for it, or I can refuse to believe you.

It is something like this with God and us. God has spoken to us through the Patriarchs and the Prophets of the Old Testament; and he has spoken to us through his Son, Jesus. He has said many things to us, about himself, about us, our lives and our world. But the most important of all these things is the summary truth: "I love you. . . . If a mother were to forget the child of her womb, I would never forget you. . . . I have always loved you from all eternity; this is why I created you. . . . I could have made a world without you, but no world would have been complete for me without you."

It is the caption under the whole life, death and resurrection of Jesus: "This is what I mean when I say 'I love you!' " The word *Gospel* means "good news." And our Gospels really bring us good news: the good news of God's eternal, unconditional love, the good news that we are the brothers and sisters of a loving Father, the good news that we have an eternal destiny. We have it all on the word of God. It is not that it is too demanding or difficult to believe; it is almost too good to believe. All love relationships begin with and are built on an act of faith, and so faith is indeed the God connection.

The power to believe is itself the gift of God. The God, whose word comes down through the centuries to me, must be a light shining into the darkness of my understanding, a reassuring hand in my hand, a loving touch on the face of my loneliness. Only God can make a believer. Only God can draw me to this moment of truth and peace.

It is frightening to know that I can refuse this gift, or be so shallow in my "yes" that I will rarely use the gift in my daily life. At the same time it is exciting to think that I can open more and more to grace, say an ever-deeper "I believe," until the circle of God becomes the one all-encompassing frame for my world picture.

"Lord," I pray, "I do believe."

Jesus: Our Comfort and Challenge

A famous psychiatrist once suggested that there are three parts of loving: kindness, encouragement, and challenge. When we really love another, we offer all three of these love-gifts. The real problem in loving is knowing when more kindness or more encouragement is needed, and deciding the right and ripe moment for challenge.

In my reading of the Gospels, I see Jesus loving in this way: sometimes offering pure kindness, sometimes encouraging others to believe in their own God-given gifts, but always and to everyone offering the love-gift of challenge: "Come, follow me! Take up your mat and walk. Believe in me!" I think that Jesus, the same yesterday, today, and always, enters our lives in just that way. If we know only the comfort of Jesus and have not felt challenged by him, we have not known the whole Jesus; we have not heard his whole message.

The first and fundamental challenge of Jesus is always that of faith. "Believe in me. . . . I am sent from the Father to teach you. . . . I am the way, the truth and the life. . . . If you follow me, you will not walk in darkness. . . . Only if you accept me and my message can you be truly free because only the truth can set you free. . . . I am the vine and you are the branches. . . . I am the Bread of Life come down from heaven so that you might have life to the full."

This was the trust and the surrender of faith with which Jesus continually challenged his slow-to-believe Apostles. They had their own dreams and plans, their own ideas about success, their own formulas for living well. They wanted God to support them, to approve their ideas and to bless their plans. But they found it hard (as we do) to surrender to a higher wisdom, to follow a call into unknown places, to be still and know that God is God.

The Apostles were reluctant to give up the driver's seat, to let go of the steering wheels of their own lives. Slowly, persistently, Jesus presented the challenge of faith: "Seek first the Kingdom of God. . . . Let go and let God have his way in your life." This challenge of faith, this letting go and letting God, this turning of our lives over to the plans and formulas of a higher wisdom is no simple matter, is it?

It is something like signing a blank check and handing it over to God, to let him fill in all the amounts: of success and failure, of joy and sorrow, even the number of days of our lives. Only a deep and trusting faith can make such a surrender. We could never do this if we did not believe that God loves us more than any mother ever loved her child.

The same challenge of Jesus is upon us: "Believe in me. . . . Seek first the Kingdom of God. Let go and let God have his way in your life. . . . Only the truth can set you free." We tremble and try to turn away. Like the Apostles we too have our plans and hopes, our formulas for a full life. We want to confront Jesus, to ask him what will happen to us if we say, "Yes!" What will I have? Will I have enough? Enough security, enough money, enough food and clothes and housing? Will I have enough strength?

The challenging Jesus understands and comforts our fear. He reassures us: "Peace will be my gift to you. . . . I will be your enough!"

Faith: A Gift to Be Used

Have you ever wondered, as I have, why some people believe and others do not? If it were a matter of intelligence or logic, I suppose that all the smart people would be believers and the less than bright would be nonbelievers. But, as we know, this is not so. Some intelligent and seemingly good people struggle all their lives without ever coming to this religious faith.

All Christian theologians are in agreement about one thing: Religious faith is a gift of God. Faith in general implies taking the word of someone for something we can't prove. If I tell you that I am five-foot-nine, you can prove it by measuring me. No need for an act of faith. But if I tell you I love you, you have to take it on faith. There is no way I can prove that I love you. This demands human faith.

God's word, beginning with his communication to Abraham in about 1850 B.C. and ending with Jesus and his Apostles, comes to us in the book we call the Bible. The main thing that God is saying to us in the Bible is precisely this: "I love you." There is no way to prove it; no way to prove that God is our Father who will never forget us, "even if a mother should forget the child of her womb." There is no way to prove that God so loved us that he became human and died on a cross for love of us.

But if there is no way to prove all this, why do we believe it? This is where the gift comes in. God has to give us the grace and ability to believe. He has to convince us: "It's really true. I do love you." Of course, God can put ideas into our minds or convictions into our hearts. Most of us have experienced God's grace in us and in our lives. One difficulty in explaining this act of God in us is that God comes to each of us in a unique way. He doesn't literally whisper inside us that it is all true. But, for example, he lets us be touched by the deep faith of someone else and uses this occasion to empower our minds to believe. God's time of grace may come while we are trying to pray or even while crossing a street. In a million different ways God seems to make us believers. But this much is clear: Only God by his grace can make us believers.

On our part we have to be ready and open to God. There are a thousand obstacles to such readiness, some of which involve human responsibility, other obstacles which may be a matter of prejudice learned early in life. But we cannot judge anyone. Maybe God is waiting to have his hour in the lives of people who are struggling with the question of belief. I do trust that God will honor all human sincerity, even if the person is so brainwashed that faith becomes difficult or impossible for his or her comprehension.

It is also true that even we who do believe still have recurrent doubts. Sometimes we experience genuine faith crises. One great theologian once said that old forms of faith are eaten away by doubt, but only so that newer and deeper forms of faith may be born in us. A psychologist named John Hinton did a study on the support and consolation of religious faith to the dying. He concluded that insofar as people had integrated faith into their daily lives, they were to that extent supported and consoled by faith in their dying. The important truth here is that faith must be regarded as a gift to be used. It grows in us only when we use it. And the more we use it the more it grows. I must use my faith or it will die.

Faith can be the motive of any action, no matter how insignificant. I can mop floors, wash dishes, or take a walk for the love of God. He wants us to be happy and filled with life. Consequently, all our efforts to be fully human and fully alive persons can become integrated acts of faith. God also wants us to love everyone, even those who are not very lovable, so that our efforts to be loving persons should be consciously motivated by faith.

Would you sometime today go back over the recent weeks in your own life, as I have done so often, and try to list the faith-motivated, faith-colored actions in those weeks? And when we do whatever we were going to do anyway, shouldn't we try to consciously do it for the love of God?

Getting the Grace of Faith

Once, at the end of a long day on the road, Jesus was sitting around a fire with his Apostles. He asked them: "Who do you say that I am?" Peter, who almost always spoke first, answered: "Jesus, you are the Messiah and the Son of God."

The Lord smiled at Peter and assured him: "You have been very blessed, Peter. Human intelligence alone could not have known this. My Father has given you this realization."

Do you remember a time in your life when the realization of something very wonderful dawned on you? You just knew that some special person really loved you. The moment of faith is like that. It is God's gift of realization that his word is really true and his love is very real.

The gift is often experienced as the "touch" of God. "He touched me and suddenly nothing seemed the same!" Human intelligence cannot come to this moment or produce this experience without a very special help from God. Faith is, from beginning to end, God's gift.

But there are things we can do to be more open to this grace. Archbishop Anthony Bloom, once a practicing physician and resolute atheist, gave this advice to a woman seeking the experience of God: "When you leave here, go out and experience this beautiful day as much as you can. And try to be aware of all that is going on inside you. Feel the sunlight on your back and the joys that stir within. Feel the breeze brushing lightly against your face and listen to your own gentle thoughts. Smell the fragrance of the flowers and hear the birds singing for you. Above all, open your heart in love to those who are close to you."

After a while the good lady came back to the archbishop and gratefully told him that she had indeed felt the presence of God in the world about her and the touch of God on the heart within her.

Most theologians would support the advice of the bishop. They propose that there are two main paths leading to the experience of God and the moment of faith (Get ready for two big words): *self-appropriation* and *self-transcendence.* Self-appropriation means self-knowledge, a deep awareness of one's senses and bodily reactions, one's emotional hungers and hurts, a consciousness of one's deepest drives and desires.

Most of us think we know ourselves, but it is only the tip of the iceberg. Dag Hammarskjold once suggested that the longest journey is the journey inward, and the most difficult exploration is that of one's own inner spaces.

We usually pretend so much in our dealings with others that we begin to believe our own pretenses. We wear so many masks and play so many roles we lose some of our ability to tell fact from fiction. We wonder who we really are.

Self-transcendence moves in the opposite direction. It means getting beyond oneself, loving another person as much as or more than we love ourselves, wanting the happiness of another as much as we want our own happiness.

No one can make these two journeys, the one inward and the other outward, without offering God a port of entry into his or her life. Whoever begins these journeys is certainly headed for an encounter with our loving God, and will certainly experience God's touch.

Several years ago, a former student of mine, Tommy, the resident atheist in my Theology of Faith course, lay dying. He had asked me, at the end of the course: "Do you think I will ever find God?" I replied: "No, Tommy, but he will find you."

His last words to me were: "We do not find God. He finds us in his own time and in his own way. Only when I opened myself in love to those around me did God come in through the door of the heart I had left open."

Somehow I think it is that way with all of us.

Thanks, Tommy.

Where on Earth Is God?

A surprising number of people think that God set the world on its course, gave it laws, and has done nothing more. Thomas Jefferson, for one, felt sure of that. In fact, he cut out of his Bible all the passages that even implied God's interaction in human events.

I think those who have actually *experienced* the touch of God in their lives believe in it, while those who have never experienced it will conclude that it is simply a myth. I myself do believe in it because I am certain that I have felt his touch in my own life.

I remember leaving for the seminary and saying good-bye to an elderly neighbor who had been good to us children. I remember my astonishment when he told me how disappointed he was that I was going into the seminary! With a troubled look, he explained: "There is no God."

Like many of us, he had experienced much sadness in his life and could not see how a God of love could preside over such a troubled world. I didn't want our last parting to become an argument, so I simply thanked him for all his kindness and wished him well.

Even for a moment I did not believe that he might be right, so I did not think too much about his remark. Then I entered the Jesuit novitiate, which was both spartan and rigorous. We wore long black cassocks and knelt to pray on wooden kneelers two or three hours a day. We rose at 5:00 in the morning and were in bed by 9:00 each night. Except for two half-hour periods of recreation, we spoke in Latin and addressed each other as "Carissime," which is roughly translated from the Latin as "Dearly Beloved." It felt like a Marine Corps boot camp.

In the midst of all this, I felt shaken suddenly by doubt about God's existence. My old friend's words had come back. In retrospect, I now understand when we put a new weight on the foundation of our faith, we have to develop a stronger faith to support the new burden. Here I was shaken by the sudden question: "What if there really *is* no God?" If this were true, I couldn't think of a more miserable way to spend my life.

For months, I agonized over this question. God seems to let questions hollow out a place inside us before he fills our emptiness with his answers. I remember watching the faces of the other novices as they prayed in chapel. They all looked so devout and pious, and there I was with only emptiness inside. I wondered if they knew something that I didn't.

Then one night at the beginning of night prayers God touched me! With the suddenness of lightning, I felt the presence of God inside of me. It was a warm springtime after a long, hard, cold winter. I felt like a balloon blown up with the ecstasy of God's love.

It was an experience that transformed the novitiate from a boot camp into a little heaven on earth. If I were ever again to deny the existence of God, I would have to deny the reality of that moment and that experience.

Of course, there have been other questions and new difficulties, new periods of darkness and new moments of grace. But it seems to be a fact that much of reality can be known only by experience.

We can't know what chocolate ice cream tastes like until we eat some. And somehow I think it is true that we can't really know the tenderness and faithfulness of God's love until we have somehow experienced his touch in our lives.

Connecting with God

Some people say they find God to be silent and distant, but others say they regularly experience the presence and power of God in their lives.

So what must a person do or be in order to be open to the experience of God? What are the dispositions needed for genuine religious experience?

The first attitude, I believe, is to realize that God is other. In the Bible God commands us: "Be still and know that I am God. My thoughts are not your thoughts and my ways are not your ways."

When we were born, we thought we were all of reality. Then in the first year of our lives we discovered that there were other people who were not a part of us. Most of us have a terrible time mastering this mystery of otherness. Something in us wants everyone to march to our drums. And the most different being of all is our great mysterious God who brought us into being and who loves us far more than we can ever know.

All of us have asked God difficult questions. One woman said to me, "Do you know what I want to ask God when I get to heaven? EVERYTHING!" We laughed, but we both understood. We are small birds flying in the great skies of God's infinite mysterious being. When we ask the questions that arise in our finite minds, God often replies with only a gentle, soft "Trust me."

The second preparation to ready ourselves for the experience of God is the disposition of surrender. I once read about a hospitalized woman who was told by her doctor that her liver had stopped functioning and she was dying. She was very sad and furious and was obsessed with the need to "tell God off."

When she struggled down to the chapel, she collapsed alone in the semidarkness and fell to the floor. When she looked up, she could see only the words on the carpet steps to the sanctuary: "Lord, be merciful to me, a sinner."

Then she related how all she could say over and over were those words: "Lord, be merciful to me, a sinner." And in her darkness, God spoke to her: "You never really turned over your whole life to me. This is what this moment in your life is all about. It is my request for surrender." And she said her life was changed by that ordeal. She knew she had to get out of the driver's seat and turn over the direction of her life to God.

A third need is for a sense of balance between two seemingly opposed things. First there must be in us a real sense of ego desperation. We have to know in the marrow of our bones that we cannot make it without God. We must know that we are dependent creatures, and that everything we have is God's gift.

The other side may sound like a denial of that dependence. But, equally so, we must have a sense of confidence in our own personal capacities—in the gifts already given to us—and we must use those gifts boldly. This is the delicate balance of the Christian.

The final condition of readiness for God is that we make our lives acts of love. "Whoever abides in love abides in God." When we choose love as a life-principle and motivation, we set up the necessary channels of God's grace to come streaming into our lives. I have a sign on the wall of my room to remind me of this great truth: "When we love—God acts!"

The greatest commandment is to love the Lord our God with everything we've got. When we set our lives on this course, the way is cleared for God to enter our lives and to use us as his instruments.

Learning to Converse
with God

Many of the saints have described prayer as a "conversation with God." When I first heard this description of prayer many years ago, my immediate question was, "Conversation is a two-way street. How can I talk to God if he doesn't talk to me?"

Every relationship is as good as its communication. This is true of our human relationships and of the relationship we have with God. The word "communicate" means to share something with another. When you and I truly communicate, you get to know me through my sharing, and I get to know you through your sharing. Our common possession is ourselves.

In this way, prayer is a conversation or communication with God. In prayer we should gradually open up more of ourselves to God. And we should get to know God better. Someone might ask: What can we say that God doesn't already know? Doesn't he know the very words we choose even before we choose them? Yes. But these questions miss the point. We don't speak to God to inform him, but to become real before him.

Speaking to God means describing ourselves as we really are. Of course, we aren't fully aware of everything that is going on in us. But the more we try to share who we really are with God, the more we will get in touch with the hidden parts of ourselves. Personal prayer has suffered because most of us read prayers or say what we think God would like to hear. The reluctant prophet Jeremiah complained to God, "You didn't make a prophet out of me. You made a fool out of me." And Job told God: "I am so miserable that I curse the day you made me." Even Jesus cried: "My God, my God, why have you forsaken me?" These are honest prayers.

How does God speak to us? The Bible is filled with stories of God communicating with believers. And God is the same yesterday, today, and always. He has equipped us with five different reception antennas through which he speaks to us: our minds, wills, imaginations, emotions, and memories.

First the mind: Have you ever thought of something and felt that the thought was put there by God? I often pray for enlightenment. I ask God to help me know what I should do or say to help someone. I always pray before I write, asking God to direct my thoughts. God has often inspired me and helped me to see things in a larger perspective.

The second channel through which God communicates with us is the will. It is in our wills that we occasionally experience strength that is not ours. It is God's strength. And I think God often gives us power to do something special.

Then there is the interior sense called the imagination. If I were to ask you to close your eyes and see a familiar face or hear a familiar voice, you would be able to do so because of the power of imagination. God can likewise put scenes or sounds into our imaginations.

There is also the channel of our emotions. God can put peace or even disturbances into our emotions. As someone has said, "God comes to comfort the afflicted, and to afflict the comfortable." In general, God's actions in us result in peace. But he may make us uncomfortable until we take up the challenge that he is holding out before us.

The final human channel God uses with us is the memory. God may remind us of his tenderness in the past. God also heals our memories when he helps us to reevaluate past experiences and to transform hurtful into helpful memories.

One last problem remains. How can I know if my thoughts, desires, imagination, feelings, and memories are really from God? Most often, there is no sure way to tell. But grace always manages to do its work. The thought or desire comes back; the hurtful memories are healed. If some enlightenment seems to involve a life-changing decision, it should be taken back again and again to prayer for confirmation. It's something like the blind man whose eyes Jesus touched several times. Each time he did, the man could see more clearly.

Finding the Will of God

One of the most moving Gospel scenes portrays Jesus agonizing in the Garden of Gethsemane. He begs his Father to spare him the suffering that is slowly closing in. In the end he says: "Nevertheless, Father, not as I will but do in me and through me whatever you will for me."

It is clear to me that the same loving God has chosen you and me for a very special purpose. God sent each of us into this world to do something that only we can. We have a special and highly personal message to deliver and a unique act of love to bestow.

Does this mean God has a specific will for *each* and *every* one of our choices? For many reasons I am sure that this is not the case. Our loving Father God knows that we have to learn how to think for ourselves and make our own choices. He knows that this is the only way we can grow into the free and fully alive persons he wants us to be.

I believe that God has a general will for us which perhaps could be expressed this way: "Make your life an act of love!" God wants us to make love the guiding force of all our decisions and the motive behind all our actions.

This general will of God is clearly a part of the teachings of Jesus: "By this shall others know that you are my disciples, by the fact that you love one another."

Still, there are times in our lives when God has a *specific* will for us. Most of us go through life making our own plans and then asking God to make them come true instead of asking God what his plans are and asking him to enlighten us about our part in those plans. But God has sent you and me into this world to do something that only we can. To remind myself, I have a sign on my mirror which reads: "Thank you for loving me, Jesus. What have you got going today? I'd like to be a part of it." That prayer represents my ideal.

When God has something specific for us, he tries to direct us by the impulse of his grace. I imagine it this way: I see myself going through a long corridor, trying to be a loving person. There are a lot of doors along this corridor but they are all closed. Then suddenly I arrive at one which is open and God nudges me with his grace. He gently points out the door and gently asks me to go through it.

To know these times and to know the specific will of God presumes a real desire and eagerness to be and do whatever he wills. All of us experience some deep fear of this surrender to God. We are afraid of what he will ask of us, like signing a blank check and worrying about whether we will be overdrawn—whether we will have enough time, strength, and courage. We are like Jesus in the Garden, and God assures us, "I will be your enough."

To do God's will is also possible only if it is built on two other convictions. I have to believe that God loves me more than I love myself and that he wants my happiness more than I want it. And I have to believe that God knows more than I do about what will make me truly happy.

I have a feeling that if God had given me everything I ever asked for, I would now be seriously unhappy. I think that one basis of my desire to find and do God's will should be this: his will is my only chance to be truly and lastingly happy.

Yes, our lives are in God's hands. And when those special moments arrive when we are to deliver our message and bestow our special act of love, God will speak to our hearts. The important thing is to cultivate *listening* hearts.

A Time for Self-renewal

Did you ever wonder where we got the word *Lent?* My dictionary says it's from an Old English word, "lencten," which means springtime. I would guess that the connection is that Lent usually comes in spring.

I always associate this time with new growth. Springtime is when the new grass, leaves, and flowers put in their first appearance of the year. Springtime is also a time of house-cleaning. It's a time for decisions: what to save and what to throw out, what to plant and where to weed.

Self-renewal is like that. It is a time for planting and a time for uprooting. As Christians in search of growth, we review our way of living, our values, and our actions to make sure they somehow reflect our faith.

I would suggest that we take each week of Lent to work on the following six life-practices to improve and renew our lives. Take one each week and work on it every day.

First: "Be a friend to yourself instead of a critic." Critics judge us; they can put us down. But friends affirm all that is good in us, and they try to understand our limitations. They work to see that our legitimate needs are fulfilled. So make a list of all the things you like about yourself.

Read it often and add to it as an exercise in self-appreciation. Also list the limitations you want to understand. Finally, ask yourself about your needs: Are you getting enough sleep, food, exercise, relaxation, and quiet time?

Second: "Be an owner not a blamer." Owners take full responsibility for their lives. They are actors, not reactors. Blamers shift the responsibility for their lives and actions onto some other person, place, or thing.

Third: "Be a sharer not a keeper." The things we share with others are somehow disarmed from hurting us. The things we keep inside fester like a splinter that is pushed under the flesh. "We are as sick as we are secret," poet John Berryman once wrote.

Fourth: "Be a forgiver not a grudge bearer." The surest way to become a slave is to resent another person. Grudges interfere with sleep, digestion, and general health. Forgiving frees not only the debt owed us but also frees *us* from the chains of resentment.

Fifth: "Enjoy life; don't just endure it." Make a list of your favorite memories at the end of each day. If you can't think of anything, you must have missed a lot of life's pleasures: sights, sounds, tastes, music and poetry, people and laughter. Did you ever think that God may wonder why we don't enjoy all the good things that he has given us? The Talmud claims that we will all have to account for the legitimate pleasures we failed to enjoy.

Sixth: "Make prayer a central part of your life." Remember the play *Harvey,* where this fellow was always talking to a nine-foot rabbit? Well, our Lord promises to be with us, helping us as we move along through life. The hardest part of life is doing it alone. But when the conversation of prayer is woven into the fabric of our lives, it's we, we, we . . . not I, I, I. Prayer releases the peace, power, and tangible presence of God into our lives.

Of course, these six exercises can be undertaken at any time of the year or at any time of life, but the six weeks of Lent sound like a good time to begin. The rest of life will be a lot easier. Life works if we will work at it.

Change a Habit—and Life!

Many students of human nature believe that the most powerful of all influences is habit. All we need are a few repetitions. Then the groove, or habit, becomes a permanent part of us.

Habits are a way of relieving the mind of having to sort through a lot of information in the process of making a decision. We do "habitual things" by rote. We don't even have to think about them. We take showers, eat meals, go to school or to work without having to think it through each time.

We have to reflect for only a moment to realize the power of habits in our lives: smoking, eating too much, losing our tempers, and failing to pray are some. We may also have positive habits like being on time, saying grace before meals, and going to Mass. An anonymous poet put the force of habit this way: "Our yesterdays lie heavily upon our todays and our todays lie heavily upon our tomorrows."

The trick is getting into the right habit. As someone once simply put it: "Begin. The rest is easy." You just have to stay in the groove.

I remember reading an article entitled "Three Weeks to a New Habit." It seems that the author realized the importance of affirmation and decided to affirm her husband every day. After three days she thought she had run out of material. Then, just before the fourth day was over, she thought of something else. It made all the difference— a real breakthrough.

Things were fine after that. Her husband and her marriage were transformed. The author assured her readers that it takes only three weeks of repetition before a person develops a habit. After that, the habit takes over.

The season of Lent is a good time to look at the habits in our lives. Saint Ignatius of Loyola said that only those who are willing to endure His suffering with Jesus will understand and enter into the glory of His Resurrection.

Perhaps, like me, you remember the days when we "gave up" something for Lent. Remember terms like "mortification" and "abnegation"? Self-denial was proposed as calisthenics are to athletes. If you're "in condition," you don't get hurt in the big game. During Lent we gave up things we enjoyed in order to strengthen our wills. That way we hoped we wouldn't get hurt in the big game of life.

Then somebody reversed the flow of that stream, suggesting that we do something *positive* rather than "giving up" some pleasure. So we started attending Mass daily or we added some extra time for prayer in our busy lives. Or we resolved to affirm a family member every day.

But this is like a diet which someone once wisely advised against: "Never go on a diet because one day you will go off it and gain back all the weight you lost. What you have to do is to begin a new way of life." In other words: "Cultivate a new habit that will be with you the rest of your life."

Obviously the spirit and time of Lent is ideal for this. Decide on something you'd like to do or be. Then practice that habit daily. It will soon become a part of you. If it really does take three weeks to form a new habit, the six weeks of Lent are ideal.

Beginning the practice of a new habit this Lent could mean a new life. Then Easter will take on a deeper, more joyful experience. And so will the rest of your life.

Change a habit and you can change life.

Suffering: Bitter or Better?

Besides taxes and death, one other inevitable reality of life is suffering. Life seems to hurt some of us very much and others less. But pain affects us all.

Some of us seem to become better human beings as a result of our suffering. I don't think Helen Keller, for example, would have become the great woman she was if it had not been for her affliction.

For most of us, however, pain seems to lead to despair and a slow self-destruction. Often our complaints turn into anger and spurt out in acts of emotional or physical violence.

In his well-known *Imitation of Christ,* Thomas à Kempis maintains that suffering can become an embittering experience. But he also suggests that if we perceive suffering as potentially valuable, we will profit from it. If we see suffering in a purely negative light, we will be destroyed by it.

Someone has suggested that the greatest blessings come into our lives disguised as problems. But we really have to work at cultivating this attitude toward adversity. "Whenever the pupil is ready," the saying goes, "the teacher will appear." When we look for the blessings hidden in adversity, we will find them.

I would like to suggest three benefits that suffering confers upon us. The first is that, if we work at developing the right attitude, suffering always deepens our trust in God.

I once had a good friend who had a coronary heart attack in his mid-thirties. George was so weakened that he could walk only short distances and had to live a sedentary life. Then in his forties George had more than twenty operations for cancer of the face, including removal of his nose.

I once asked George if he ever wondered why he had to live with so much infirmity. I will never forget his answer: "These are the cards God lovingly dealt me, and these are the cards I will lovingly play." I will always be grateful for the deep trust in God's wisdom which those words revealed.

The second blessing suffering offers is a signal that there is something wrong in our lives.

"Thank God for your pain," urges Dr. Paul Brand, who has worked most of his life in leper colonies. Lepers lose all sensation, so they have no pain to warn them, Dr. Brand explains. Their fingers may drop off because they have no pain to alert them to infection. "Pain is always telling you something if you are willing to listen."

Knotted stomachs and tension headaches, for example, warn us that we are looking at something in a self-destructive way. If we didn't have physical, emotional, and social discomfort to remind us, we might go on trying to be what we can never be, to do what we can never do.

Finally, suffering gives us a sense of who we are and what life is all about. By definition, a pilgrim is a person making a journey to a holy place. Well, we are on our way to God's house, which will be our home forever. Suffering always reminds us that—like pilgrims—we are not yet home.

The dark and difficult days in our lives remind us that we must surrender to total trust in God . . . that we are pilgrims on our way to a holy place, God's house . . . and that we may not be enjoying the journey, as God wants us to, if we try to do or be what's unrealistic.

So let's pray for each other that we will both find the promise in every problem, the many blessings that come into our lives disguised as serious problems.

Faith: A New Vision

An old Roman philosopher named Epictetus used to go around challenging people who were sad, angry, riddled with fears: "It's all in the way you look at it. You'd better take another look!"

And we are all familiar with the couplet: "Two men looked out from prison bars. One saw mud and one saw stars."

Then there is that cute ditty reminding us: "As you ramble through life, my brother, my sister, whatever be your goal, keep your eye upon the doughnut and not upon the hole."

Some people look at a glass of water and moan: "Oh, it's half empty!" Others look at the same glass and rejoice: "Gee, it's half full!"

Psychologists are sure our emotional and behavioral reactions are not caused by the persons and events in our lives, but rather by our interpretation or evaluation of those persons and events. It all depends on the way we look at them. In other words, the same event can either be disastrous or a challenge to grow, depending on how we look at it. We make our own experiences from the materials that life supplies.

Psychologists are not sure who is seeing reality correctly. The saint sees others as brothers and sisters, the image and likeness of God. Is the saint—someone like Mother Teresa of Calcutta—naive? The cynic sees others as selfish, suspicious. Who is right? Are we a human family, or is it the survival of the fittest? The psychologist doesn't know.

When John the Baptist began his preaching on the banks of the Jordan, the burden of his message was *metanoia:* a change of outlook! Open your minds and hearts. God has spoken his word into the world and it's going to change everything!

Then Jesus came to the Jordan, just as he comes into our lives, to change everything. To those who protested that they were free, Jesus cautioned: "No, you are not free until you accept me and my message. Your tyrants are not outside you, but inside you—the tyranny of fear, guilt, anger, the grudges you bear. Only the Truth can set you free. I am sent from the Father for your liberation, to bring you the Truth."

I once knew a man who suffered from extreme myopia, or nearsightedness. When schools sent home the report of this to his parents, they dismissed the warnings. They did not need glasses at his age. Why should he?

So my friend stumbled along in a world of mist. He interpreted everything according to what he could see— for example, the notes of the teacher on the chalkboard. Since he couldn't read them, he deduced that she put them there as notes for herself, so she would know what to say.

And why were street signs placed so high that no one could read them? Ah! So the bus drivers, who sit high up in the buses, can read them and tell others where they were. He deduced that baseball was such a difficult sport because the batter or the catcher could see the ball only a few feet away.

Then one day, as a young adult, he went to an eye doctor, who fitted him with corrective lenses and invited him to look out the window. Oh, wow! He could see the blue sky, the white clouds, the green leaves, the shafts of sunlight, the hues of so many colors! It was magnificent.

My friend tells me that it was the second most beautiful moment of his life. The most beautiful? "The day I invited Jesus to be the Lord of my life. The day I said 'yes' to his vision, his evaluation of things. I saw the world through his eyes, and everything looked different. It was magnificent.

"I am like the blind man in the Gospels who was given vision gradually by the repeated touches of the hand of Jesus. I feel something of his ecstasy when he kept saying: 'All I know is that once I was blind and now I can see!' "

"Jesus, Son of David, please touch my eyes, too."

Faith: Our Attitudes
and the BE-attitudes

The brilliant philosopher-psychologist William James once declared: "The greatest discovery in our generation is that human beings, by changing the inner attitudes of their minds, can change the outer aspects of their lives."

I am absolutely convinced that our attitudes are the control centers of our lives. They regulate our emotions, our health, our relationships, and the use of our talents.

I am also sure that all change, growth, and conversions must begin in our attitudes. If there is a change in attitude, it will affect all the aspects of our lives: our emotions, health, relationships, use of talent. If there is no change in attitude, there is no real change at all.

But first, what is an attitude? It is a way of looking at something, a way of thinking about something, which we have practiced until that way of thinking has become a habit.

An attitude is a practiced way of regarding something. To change an attitude is to break an old habit and learn a new one. We have thousands of attitudes in our minds, one for everything that we have experienced or know about. We have attitudes toward ourselves, our bodies, our personalities, other people, life and death, success and failure, pain and pleasure, money, power, and so forth.

What does an attitude do? When anything happens in our lives, the message or stimulus comes through our senses into our minds, and then one of our attitudes interprets, evaluates, and pronounces judgment; it also prescribes an appropriate reaction to the happening or experience.

This interpretation and evaluation of the attitude determines everything else: our emotional reaction, our bodily reaction, and our subsequent behavior.

For example, you look into the mirror and discover you are growing old. New gray hairs, new wrinkles. Now, you have an attitude inside you about growing old. This attitude then interprets and judges the evidence seen in the mirror. Your feelings are determined by this interpretation and judgment.

You might feel pleased, knowing that all real life begins at forty, or in the words of Robert Browning: "Grow old along with me! The best is yet to be." Or you may groan with grief: "Just when I got over the hump, I'm also over the hill!"

So you smile or you cry, but it all depends on your attitude. All your reactions and behavior depend on your attitudes. If you are happy, it is a good indication that you have healthy attitudes. If you are sad, sick, lonely, not realizing your potential, it is quite certain that there are one or more crippling, destructive attitudes in you.

When Jesus encountered people, he constantly asked them to look at their attitudes, constantly challenged them to revise those attitudes that were keeping them small-sad persons living in a small-sad world.

He was saying something like this: "Your tyrants are inside you, in the distorted attitudes that result in greed, lust, hatred, pride. Change your outlook. Let the Truth set you free. Believe in me. I will show you a completely new vision of reality.

"I will give you a new pair of eyes, the eyes of faith. These are the BE-attitudes, the attitudes that will lead you to the fullness of life and bring you to peace of soul. I am calling you to life, to joy!"

The real imitation of Christ begins with taking his mind, his way of seeing things, his attitudes, and making them our own. This involves a study of the Gospels, reading about the life and mind of Jesus. But above all, it involves a life of prayer, a running conversation with the Lord of life through all the days and cycles of life.

"Jesus, call me out of my darkness into your light. Call me out of my blindness into your sight. Call me out of my loneliness into your love."

The Christian Attitude toward Self

There is little doubt that the most important judgment you or I will ever make in the course of our lives is the judgment we will make about ourselves.

Of all the many attitudes inside us by far the most decisive is the attitude we have about ourselves. Whatever we think about ourselves more than any other factor influences how we feel, how we relate to others, what we try, and what we desire and expect from life.

Low self-esteem is a vicious trap. When we get caught in this trap, we send out the message to other people (with or without words), and they treat us accordingly. We instruct them (with or without words) not to esteem us, to ignore us, to forget us, to interrupt us, to walk over us. And when they do these things, we are confirmed in our original low self-esteem. A vicious trap and a vicious circle.

Also, to the extent that we do not love ourselves, we do not love anyone else, including God! When we think poorly of ourselves, we feel the sharp edges of self-contempt, the quiet desperation of emptiness, personal bankruptcy. The great psychiatrist Carl Jung says that when we do not love ourselves, there is a constant "civil war" instead of a "celebration" going on inside us. And this war and this pain absorb all our attention. We have little or no attention and availability for others, except to use them and ask them to make us feel better. Did you ever have a throbbing toothache? Do you remember whom you were thinking about? (Yourself and the dentist, right?)

Jung says that we all know what Jesus said about "the least of my brethren." But what, he asks, if you were to discover that the least of the brethren of Jesus, the one person who most needs your love is . . . you? Would you get a high place in heaven if you were judged only on how well you have loved, understood, and appreciated yourself?

Does God really want us to love ourselves? There is no doubt that he does! Jesus asked us to love our neighbors as we love ourselves. Saint Ambrose of Milan, in the fourth century, wrote that humility does not mean self-depreciation ("I'm a sewer . . . I'm a sewer!") It means acknowledging all the good and beautiful things God has lovingly done in us, and then praising God for his goodness.

He says that the perfect expression of humility in the New Testament is in the words of Mary, the Mother of Jesus, when she cries out to her cousin Elizabeth: "My soul makes much of the Lord, and my spirit leaps for joy in God my Savior. He has graciously looked upon his little servant-girl, and from this day forth age after age will call me blessed! He who is mighty has done great things in me. Holy is his name."

Low self-esteem is like a hand brake on a car. The lower the self-esteem the slower we move. Our God-given talents can't flow. We cannot move into meaningful relationships. It's so crippling we have to ask: How do we ever get into this trap?

Well, there are messages on the tapes that play constantly in our heads, messages from significant people in our lives (low self-esteem is contagious). These messages may tell us that looks or brains or education is everything! They may tell us that we are not lovable or capable. But remember this: It isn't what they say to you that really counts. It's what you are saying to yourself.

What should you be saying to yourself?

"I am the child of God's heart, carved on the palm of his hand. He resides in my heart with great delight. I am a unique and unrepeatable image and likeness of God. There never was and never will be another me!"

You see, that is what God thinks of you. To hate yourself would almost be blasphemy!

What's in an Old Memory?

Everyone is familiar with the saying: "Today's experiences—tomorrow's memories." And that would be a consoling thought, except that many memories are painful for us. Like old thorns under the flesh, they fester inside us.

The worst part about our painful memories is they keep us locked up in a painful prison, unable to live and love as God intended for us.

I know many people who had a miserable childhood and feel doomed to a miserable life. They carry around inside of them very painful memories such as the experience of feeling rejected by others, wetting their pants in school, being humiliated by teachers, and so forth. Later in life were broken romances and broken trusts, shattered dreams and loneliness, failures and disappointments.

Jesus said that he came that we might have the fullness of life, but with a lot of us, painful memories keep us locked inside. We hardly experience love for others or God to our fullest capacity because the pain of these memories imprisons and shackles us.

The first thing I think that we have to do is the exact opposite of trying to suppress or forget these memories.

We have to go back and relive the experience that has become a painful memory. However, we go back with the perspective that we have now. We bring the wisdom of whatever years we have to reevaluate a child's embarrassment, an adolescent failure, or an adult's rejection.

There are times when I think of my own experience of being a sad and lonely child who was treated cruelly by other children. As I dig into my own memories, I ask God to heal my old and painful scars. The process of change is always a process of God's grace.

I recall a little boy who was painfully shy. I review definite scenes in which the poor little fellow felt embarrassed, times when he cried or was bullied in the school yard. I understand him a lot better now. In these painful episodes I really want to hug him. To tell him that it's all right to cry, that I understand his sadness. I assure him that I'm not ashamed of him. And then again I pray that God will touch these painful memories and transform them into helpful memories.

I find myself wanting to reassure the poor, misunderstood little boy. I truly get to like that little fellow as a result of reliving and reevaluating what may have seemed a trivial occurrence to anyone else.

Somehow we have to do this for others as well as for ourselves. In trying to understand others, we are encouraged to listen long and carefully enough to understand the inner consistency of others.

Just like ourselves, what others do and say is consistent with the world and the experiences that have shaped them.

Only when we can understand this inner consistency between our memories and our present experiences can we truly achieve the full potential which God has placed in you and in me. Only then can we rejoice in the fullness of life that Jesus came to bring us. Only then can we really be free.

Believe in Your Beauty

There is a little rhyming goody that goes something like this: If you can conceive it and you can believe it, then you can achieve it.

I suppose it means something like this: If you can conceive something as possible and you believe in your ability to make that dream a fact, then you can, in fact, achieve your goal. Do you believe that? How would this apply to your own life?

Remember Grimm's fairytale about Rapunzel—the story of the beautiful girl who lives with an old witch in a tower? The old witch constantly tells little Rapunzel how ugly she is. In fact, the witch insists, "You look just like me!"

Since there are no mirrors in the tower, poor Rapunzel believes it. She can't see her own beauty, so she remains a prisoner in the tower . . . a prisoner of her own supposed ugliness. The witch knew that if Rapunzel were convinced of her ugliness, she would never attempt to escape from the tower.

But, alas, one bright day Prince Charming comes riding by on his white horse just as Rapunzel is leaning out of the tower for a breath of fresh air. And Prince Charming immediately stops to admire the winsome lass. After an exchange of reassuring smiles, she throws her long, blond hair out the window and the prince climbs up on a ladder of her hair into the tower. As the two of them gaze admiringly into each other's eyes, Rapunzel sees in the glistening eyes of her prince a clear reflection of her own face. In the mirror of his eyes Rapunzel sees that she really is a beauty.

And in this instant, she is free! Free from the witch! Free from the tower! Free from the fear that she is ugly! And so the couple parachutes from the tower, lands on Prince Charming's white steed, and rides off happily into the sunset.

Just like Rapunzel, all of us, to some extent, are locked inside ourselves by our fears of ugliness, inferiority, and inadequacy. As with most of our problems, this one, too, is fundamentally a problem of poor self-image.

We don't really believe that the Lord would pour his message, his song, his love into such a broken and leaking vessel. We need to be freed by the realization of our giftedness and our goodness and our beauty.

Of course, there are many examples of people in Jesus' life who felt this weakness, too. There's fumbling Peter who was named the Rock but really resembled a sandpile. There was also little Zacchaeus, the tax collector, who was up in a tree in more ways than one. And, of course, there was Mary Magdalene, out of whom the Lord had cast seven devils.

Jesus looked directly into the eyes and hearts and the lives of these people. And they, like so many of us down through the centuries, saw their own beauty reflected in his eyes.

We all have been freed from the captivity of our fears by his caring. And when we feel the echo in ourselves of Peter's words, "Oh, depart from me, Lord. I'm a sinful man. I'm not your type. I'm not good enough," Jesus simply looks at us and says, "Shalom, be at peace. I understand."

Somehow, if we feel that we are right with God, then we are all right indeed.

The Ten-Statement
Autobiography

If you wanted someone to know you as completely as possible and if you could only make ten statements to this person, what would you say?

Before God created this world he knew its every dimension. He knew there would be some sunlit moments in our lives, moments when we would feel the warmth of his presence. But he also knew there would be cold and dark days when we would have to ask for trust and endurance. And all he would promise was a happy ending for those who would be faithful.

I think of our personal qualities and gifts, our joys and sorrows, the people who enter and leave our lives, as the lumber God gives us to build our personal monuments of praise to him. Out of this lumber we will fashion either a stumbling block or a stepping stone. The critical realization is that God in his act of creation chose every detail of our lives as an act of love, so that we would in turn build monuments of praise to him. My life is really God's gift to me. What I do with it will be my gift to God.

The first of my ten statements would certainly concern the parents God gave me. I have so many memories of being loved and cared for. If our first years are really the

most important, then I was truly blessed. I especially remember my mother and her deep faith, her vision of life
and love which was a large part of my parental inheritance.
I remember the high school I attended, a school of strong
spirit and teachers who truly cared. Ideals of dedication
and commitment were inculcated into us that have lasted
and grown.

Another statement in my autobiography would be about
the personal gifts God has given me. The song in my heart
is like Mary's Magnificat: "My soul magnifies the Lord.
My spirit rejoices in God my Savior. He who is mighty has
been so good to me that everyone will call me blessed."

Saint Paul once asked, "What have you got that you
were not given?" I believe all my days have been filled
with God's blessings. I'm often invited to speak before
audiences, and sometimes their applause is hearty. While
I'm gesturing my acceptance, under my breath I'm telling
the Lord that the applause really belongs to him. I truly
have nothing that I was not given.

A third statement in my autobiography would have to
include the blessing God has given me in the form of
suffering. As I gain a little distance from some of the
suffering of my own life, I begin to see its meaning and
how much I have learned from it. In the midst of my
suffering I usually complain to God as Job once did, but
God asks me to trust him, to believe that he really wants
my happiness more than I do and that he knows what
will make me truly happy.

Sometimes my surrender has come slowly. However,
over the years I think my trust has grown deeper. I am
often reminded of the statement that sometimes our best
blessings come into our lives disguised as problems. And
often I thank God for the blessings that I have not recognized because they came in the form of a cross.

If I really wanted someone to know me, I would have to include the insights that have become my life-principles. These life-principles seem to sum up my hopes and ambitions. They give my life meaning and direction. The first of many I might mention is the desire to make my life a genuine act of love and not a performance. The psychiatrist Carl Jung once said he was most grateful for four gifts: faith, hope, love, and insight. I find an echo of his gratitude in myself.

Lastly, if you would know me, you would have to know this: I think of our lives as gigantic jigsaw puzzles. Each day God gives us a new set of pieces to fit into the picture. Some of these pieces are sharp and colorless. Our first instinct is to throw them away. But only God knows the beauty that will emerge when all the pieces are in place. We will see that beauty only when we have fitted in the last piece, the piece of our dying. It helps me to pause, to reflect about the lumber of our lives with which we can build either a stumbling block or a stepping stone.

Loving Yourself and Others, Too

Back in the second century, Saint Irenaeus wrote, "The glory of God is a person who is fully alive." He meant, I think, that the essential way we praise God and thank him is by using all his gifts. Sometimes I think God must wonder a bit about us: "Why don't you enjoy the beautiful world I've made? Why don't you like my other children? Why don't you appreciate and use my gifts to you?"

It seems most of us don't really enjoy the gift of life or live fully. Students of human nature suggest the main reason is that we don't love or even like ourselves very much. We have an inner image that is ugly and defective. We can't imagine that anyone who really knew us could love us.

Someone has wisely said that for most of us, the biblical command "Love your neighbor as yourself" should be "Love yourself and you will love your neighbor." If you hate yourself, your neighbor doesn't have a chance. If you don't appreciate the gifts of God in yourself, you won't appreciate his gifts in others.

How did we fall into this trap of self-rejection? Since our earliest years, we were compared and we compared ourselves to others. Someone probably looked at the kid in the crib next to ours and exclaimed, "Oh, what a beautiful baby," and then looked at us and said nothing. It could have started as early as that. Then we got into the comparison game ourselves. We always managed to find someone who was better looking, smarter, or who had more than we did. But when we compare ourselves with others, we lose a sense of our uniqueness. Just as no two snowflakes are identical, so each one of us is unique, an "original" by God. The package of goodness and giftedness that is you and me was never put together before and never will be again.

God alone knows us as we really are. Only his judgment really matters. And he has said: "I could have made a world without you, but no world would have been complete for me without you. I could have made you different— a queen, a king, a genius. But I didn't want you to be any of these. I wanted you to be you, because it's this you I've always loved. So please don't compare yourself to anyone else. Just know you are exactly what I want you to be."

For a believer, all this is true, and we have God's own Word for it. The real challenge is to take it in, to make it a part of us. Try this experiment: Sit down and close your eyes. Imagine an empty chair facing you. Now imagine a friend or a relative walks into the room, sits in that chair and looks at you. Register your feelings for this person. Decide what one thing you would like to say to this person, and say it. Then have a second friend or relative come out and sit in the same chair and again become conscious of your feelings. Notice they are different from your feelings for the first person. What would you like to say to this second person? Say it.

After the second person has risen and left, see a third person come in and sit in the chair. This time it's you. Try to become fully aware of all your feelings about yourself.

Notice how the imagined you sitting on the chair looks back at the real you. Is he or she happy or sad? Afraid? Braced for criticism? Then say something like this: "I'm sorry. I've never really appreciated your goodness and your giftedness. I've always been comparing you with others. From now on, I will see you through the eyes of a friend."

If you practice this genuine self-appreciation long enough, you will be a new person. You will be with someone you like twenty-four hours a day. Not much can make you unhappy. You will be more fully alive. This is the glory of God. But this glory can be achieved fully only when we fully appreciate the gift of God that is ourselves.

We recall that the psychiatrist Carl Jung once said: "We all know what Jesus said about the least of his brethren, that he takes as being done to himself whatever we do to them." Then Jung wisely asks, "But what if you were to find out that the least of his brethren—the one who needs you most and would profit most from your love—is really you?"

Count Your Blessings

Saint Ambrose once wrote that the Magnificat of Mary, the Mother of Jesus, is the perfect expression of humility.

You will remember that Mary's cousin, Elizabeth, is startled when the Mother of our Lord comes to help her. You will recall how Mary threw herself into the arms of her cousin and uttered her now well-known Magnificat.

Mary magnifies, makes much of the goodness of the Lord. She knows that her own motherhood was simply a gift of God, no achievement of her own. She also knows and says that anyone who truly knows her will have to admit that she was richly blessed by God.

"This," says Ambrose, "is the perfect expression of humility."

Humility is truth, and it starts with the truth of God's goodness to us. If I don't appreciate the goodness of his gifts, I will certainly be failing in the virtue of gratitude. Humility begins with this honest acknowledgment and it ends with a joyful hymn of gratitude and praise: "Thank you, Lord, for your countless blessings."

Now most of us would be able to recite a long list of our failures and regrets; we are painfully aware of our limitations. But if someone asked, "What do you like best about yourself?" most of us would probably stammer and stutter.

It's true we all have skeletons in our closets, blotches on our records, and weaknesses that keep coming back to haunt us. But setting out to look only for our weaknesses is the surest route to discouragement and depression. And worse, it is also blinding—it keeps us from seeing our many gifts and blessings.

With all my heart I believe that I need to know my blessings much more than I need to know my blemishes. I truly believe that my only chance to love others and to love God begins with this appreciation of my own goodness.

This appreciation accounts for the difference between cynics and saints. Saints seek and find God's goodness everywhere—in themselves and in others. We can love and appreciate others only to the extent that we love and appreciate ourselves. If we don't acknowledge God's unique gifts in ourselves, we won't appreciate his special gifts in other people.

Let me ask you to start an inventory today of everything that is good about yourself. Include everything: physical qualities like curly hair or a contagious laugh; special gifts like musical talent or athletic ability; virtues like compassion and honesty; and don't forget qualities like friendliness and enthusiasm.

Now an essential part of this exercise is to keep this list close at hand because we always find whatever we're looking for. As you start this inventory of blessings, you're going to keep discovering more and more you will need to record.

I keep a list like this myself, and it eventually became so long I had to alphabetize it. I was starting to repeat the same good qualities! I keep my list in the center drawer of my desk and I show it to others to get them started.

And one more thing—at the bottom of my list of blessings and gifts I've printed in large letters: THANK YOU, FATHER. For me, those words are the difference between a joyful humility and a blind pride.

After all, as Saint Paul wrote, what do you have that you did not receive from the Father?

The Christian Attitude
toward Others

There is an old Irish ditty that goes: "To live above with the saints we love,/Ah! that is the purest glory,/But to live below with the saints we know,/Ah! that is another story."

It's not really funny, is it? We all have some problems getting along with others, and there are some few others we just don't like. And good old Saint John reminds us that the test of our love of God is our love for one another. Then there is the haunting request of Jesus: "Love one another as I have loved you."

Somewhere deep down inside you and me is an attitude toward other people. Of course, we make careful distinctions: Some people are nice, others are not. But there is a general expectation or attitude. When we walk down a busy street or push through a crowded department store, when we walk into a room full of strangers, there is a feeling and anticipation inside us. We are secure or afraid, intimidated or cynical, sympathetic or suspicious, inclined to reach out or to run away. As difficult as it may be for us to locate and identify our fundamental attitude toward others, we really should search through our feelings to find and reexamine that attitude.

About once a month I visit a prisoner in a state penitentiary. It is difficult for me. The atmosphere is dismal and charged with suspicion. On one occasion an elderly woman and I were going through the visitors' line together. We were searched, asked to pass through metal detectors, to produce identification. The sweet, dear lady was smiling through it all, greeting everyone in a warm, loving way. Suddenly I heard myself saying to her: "Gee, I'll bet you bring a lot of love into this world, with your smiling face and words." "Father," she replied, "there are no strangers in my world. Only brothers and sisters. Some of them I haven't yet met." I had a deep feeling that she really meant it, and I remembered the advice of Charles Peguy: "Don't try to go to God alone. He will certainly ask you: 'Where are your brothers and sisters?' "

That lady drew out of me a deep and warm reaction of love. And gradually I came to realize that people are not one thing, good or bad, but many things. In every human being there is warmth, love, affection, but there is also hurt, anger, weakness. We stimulate and draw out of them one or the other. It all depends upon our approach, and our approach depends upon our attitude.

This was the genius of Jesus. He took people where they were and loved them into life. He reached into their deepest parts, found their goodness and showed it to them in the way he treated them. So little Zacchaeus, the gouging tax-collector, became an honest man. The prostitute, Mary Magdalene, became an honest and even a saintly woman.

I am reminded of those well-known words of Roy Croft: "I love you not only for what you are, but for what I am when I am with you. I love you not only for what you have made of yourself, but for what you are making of me. For passing over all the foolish, weak things that you can't help dimly seeing there, and for drawing out into the light all the beautiful belongings that no one else had looked quite far enough to find."

This is precisely what Jesus did for Zacchaeus and Mary Magdalene and for everyone whose life he touched. He was a living portrait of love in action. And the caption under the portrait reads: "Please love one another as I have loved you."

Seek the Beauty Within

Sometimes at prayer, when the candles are burning and there are flowers on the altar, it seems so easy to love others. Then when you go out of the church to find your car hemmed in by others, love and understanding don't seem to come as easily.

Most of us, I know, find it hard to live with others. We're all so different that it's difficult to put any two people together without getting some kind of disagreement or conflict.

Some people start out fast in the morning and jump out of bed saying, "Good morning, God." Others of us, on the other hand, find it hard to believe that God really created mornings.

Somehow I feel sure that we all have one thing in common—a sense of insecurity. All of us, no matter how we try to fool others, have a nagging sense of inadequacy and inferiority. We need to be affirmed or we lose our sense of worth. We need to succeed at something or we begin to feel like failures. We need others to love us or we experience loneliness.

When you think about it, all the obnoxious qualities that we observe in ourselves and in others are really cries of pain. We brag and lie only because we're trying to fill some places in ourselves that feel empty. We lash back at others because we have been hurt or neglected. We get drunk or abuse drugs because we find reality too much to bear. We get depressed because we can't let out our true feelings.

Our self-centeredness is not the result of pride but rather the result of our pain. Because pain always magnetizes our attention. When we have a toothache, the only person we can think about is ourselves and any dentist.

I remember visiting my mother at the end of her life when she was confined to a nursing home. As I was once walking down the long corridor past rows of wheelchairs and outstretched arms wanting to be touched, one of the nurses whispered to me, "Remember, Father, inside each one of these dear old ladies was once a beautiful young woman."

That remark stimulated a lot of thoughts in me. And my thoughts ended with the realization that inside each one of us is a unique image and likeness of God—a beautiful person.

I imagine it is like the case of the great Renaissance artist Michelangelo, who created the beautiful Pieta that now graces the Vatican. It is said that Michelangelo somehow saw that striking image imprisoned in the block of marble that he used.

I truly believe that there is a buried beauty in each one of us. But this beauty is often obscured by our weaknesses, our bragging, our lying, our sarcasm and cynicism. These are our disguised cries of pain, our psychological and spiritual toothaches.

All we need to call out this beauty is a little love and a little understanding. It will help us find and reveal our own goodness.

No doubt you have heard that the human brain is the most sophisticated computer ever built. It harbors quadrillions of memories and messages. We can find in ourselves the sparks of shorted fuses. But somewhere, deep within ourselves, there is a kind and gentle person. Perhaps we have never looked long enough or far enough into ourselves to discover this beauty that lies buried within each of us.

The Beauty within Us

We are all made in the image and likeness of God. The trouble is that this beauty is often obscured by our weaknesses, lying, sarcasm, and seeming self-centeredness. But these are only our masks, our disguised cries of pain.

Beneath them, hidden under all the debris of our humanness, is a little child, in need of a kind person who comes with gentleness and kindness. That child is basically simple, unsophisticated. The face of goodness is obscured by external weakness; the voice of the child is muffled by other noises.

Shortly after I was ordained I volunteered to give a retreat to other priests. I was too young and inexperienced to anticipate the difficulties, but they all became clear as I stood outside the retreat chapel and watched the other priests go in. My first shock was to notice that there were two bishops and a number of monsignors. My second shock came when I saw I was about fifteen years younger than the youngest retreatant.

The monsignor who served as the retreat house administrator asked me, "How do you feel?"

"Terrified," I said. "Did you see them?"

"Oh, they just need what everyone else needs," he laughed, "a little love and understanding."

"Why don't they look like it?" I asked. I nervously walked down the chapel aisle and led the fathers in prayer. When I faced them, I was sure I read in every face, "Where did we get this kid?" So I told a joke. There was only a long silence. At that moment, almost anything would have been preferable to giving that retreat. I stumbled through that first talk, then went back to my room wondering how I would make it through the rest of the retreat.

That night, five priests came to see me. Three of them cried tears of loneliness, sadness, and disappointment. I kept wondering. "Were you in chapel tonight?" But of course, the monsignor was right—"They're just like everyone else; all they need is a little love and understanding."

This was the way Jesus led so many out of the darkness into the light, into a peaceful world of love. I think of Mary Magdalene. Her whole life had been a disappointing search for love and understanding. Many others only wanted to use her. Then the love and kindness of Jesus drew her out of her personal darkness into the light.

During Jesus' final suffering it was this Mary Magdalene who stood out. While the Apostles remained locked in a prison of fear, she stood boldly at the foot of the cross. She must have endured taunts from those who reminded her of her past: "Come on, Mary. What's all this pious stuff? We know you." I doubt she even heard them.

Mary was only one of the many transformed by Jesus' understanding and love. The Apostles proved weak but Jesus never gave up on them. He loved them into life. His understanding and love patiently tolerated their limited grasp of his message. In the end, they left him to die alone, but after his Resurrection Jesus returned to them with a renewed promise of understanding and love: "Shalom! Be at peace. I understand." And slowly the beauty buried within them began to surface.

Likewise, I believe there really are two persons in every one of us. There is the weak and wounded person, who sometimes is the most obvious. But there is also within each of us a beautiful person—the unique image of God. All we need to call this beauty out is a little love and understanding.

Perhaps you can remember how the goodness in you surfaced and showed through when you responded to love. If you are like me, you can also remember how the hurt and defensive self surfaced and shone through when you were criticized and attacked. When we think about it, we can do either to ourselves. We can assume the role of critic. But we can also be a friend to ourselves. It may sound rather silly, but it will make all the difference in our lives.

In Giving, You Will Receive

In the thirteenth century, Saint Francis of Assisi, the little poor man of God, composed a prayer asking God to enable him to replace his hatred with love. At the end of this beautiful prayer, Francis details some of the paradoxes posed by Jesus. Among them he says that "it is in giving that we receive."

Jesus himself had a difficult time convincing the people of his time and even his own Apostles of this reality. Just think of the Last Supper when Jesus was about to wash the feet of the Apostles.

"Oh, no. You're not going to wash my feet," protested Peter. "You shouldn't be washing our feet."

But our Lord replied, "If I don't, you can't be my partner in the Kingdom."

The Kingdom of God, Jesus was saying, requires us to make our lives an act of giving, of service. "If you don't understand this," Jesus said, "you don't understand me. And if you don't understand me, you can't be my partner in the Kingdom."

Poor Peter, who almost always had footprints around his mouth, then invites Jesus to wash his hands and head, too!

Afterwards, Jesus asks: "Now you call me 'Master' and 'Lord,' but I have been trying to give you an example to follow. You should do this for others, And if you do, you will be very happy."

This truth, like many other truths, has to be experienced before it can be believed. Like the color green. Like the taste of chocolate.

I remember my experiencing this once when I volunteered to give a retreat a few years ago for a group of nuns whose order was founded to treat terminal cancer victims. All of the people they cared for were poor and could not afford personal medical care. Almost every day the sisters experienced the pain and the death of their patients. I went to the retreat expecting that these heroic sisters would be sad.

Contrary to my anticipations I found the sisters among the most joyful and happy people I have ever met. I remember that the sisters received a call during the retreat. They were told that an old lady was lying on a pile of rags, dying of cancer.

The sisters flew into motion. One whistled and a helper drove up in a remodeled hearse to take them to the poor woman. They brought her to the convent, bathed her wasted body, dressed her in silk pajamas, and laid her in a bed between clean white sheets.

Within fifteen minutes the woman was dead! I remarked that it was unfortunate she didn't live longer. "Oh, no," one sister said with a smile, "she died with dignity. And that's what we're here for.

"We treat them all as children of the King. She died between clean sheets with people praying for her. That's the way all people should die. And now she is with God, praying for us."

Before I left that convent-hospital, I asked the sisters how they could be so happy, living as they did with all the suffering and death. Again I seemed to have asked an embarrassing but obvious question. I remember that one of the sisters explained simply: "Our patients do that for us."

The retreat was preached by me to the sisters, but the lesson the sisters preached to me by their lives was much more valuable. I learned from those sisters that "it is in giving that we receive." Just as Jesus himself promised: "If you do this, you will be very happy."

The Christian Attitude toward Life

As I read the Gospels, Jesus seems to be saying that the secret of a full and satisfying life isn't found so much in what you are doing or where you are doing it but in *why* you are doing it. It is this *why*, this ultimate motive or what is called a "life-principle," that gives a human life meaning. And there is no doubt that meaning is essential to a full and satisfying life.

At the beginning of his public life, Jesus is led by the Holy Spirit into the desert. Here, after forty days of solitude and fasting, Jesus is tempted by the Devil (Luke, Chapter 4). He is tempted to pleasure (bread), power (rule over the kingdoms of the world), and to the abdication of responsibility for his own life (throwing himself off the high roof of the temple). Jesus firmly rejects all three life-principles. He will not live for pleasure or power, and he will not surrender responsibility for his own life.

By a not so strange coincidence, these three rejected life-principles are given much attention in the history of psychology. Freud and his followers believed that the ultimate drive in all of us is to pleasure. Adler broke off with Freud in suggesting that it is rather the pursuit of power that ultimately motivates mankind. We are not pleasure seekers so much as power brokers. In our own times

B. F. Skinner and many others believe that we are pro-grammed early in life. This "operant conditioning" de-prives us of the dignity of freedom to choose, and, like phonograph records, we are spinning out and acting out the messages imprinted on us in our first years.

It is probably true that some of us do choose the paths of pleasure as a life-principle; others of us are seduced by power, and no doubt many of us just give up and wait to see what life will do to us and for us. Jesus will have none of these tyrants.

All through his life, Jesus preaches and practices the only life-principle acceptable in the Kingdom of God: *love!* "By this shall everyone know that you are my disci-ples, that you love one another. Love one another as I have loved you." At the Last Supper Jesus lives out this life-principle in a very dramatic episode. Jesus begins the ritual of washing the feet of the Apostles. Peter immedi-ately objects. They all knew that the host of a dinner washed the feet only of those guests who honored him by coming to dinner, guests of higher social standing. When Peter objects, Jesus very forcefully reminds him that loving service is the only recognized life-principle in the Kingdom of God. He says equivalently: "Peter, if you don't understand this, you don't understand me, and that means that you can't be my partner in the Kingdom." The good heart of impetuous Peter then insists that Jesus wash his hands and head also. "All I want is to be with you!" he seems to be saying.

When John tells us this story of the Last Supper, he recalls that Jesus, in concluding his final instruction, says: "If you keep this in mind and put it into practice, you will be very happy."

Do I really understand? Am I committed, at all the cross-roads and in all the moments of decision, to ask: "What is the loving thing to do?" Do I really believe that love is the only way to true happiness and the fullness of life, joy, and peace promised by Jesus? The answers to these questions lie deep inside me. I must attempt some search of those deepest parts. My whole life is at stake.

What Does Life Ask of Us?

Most of us are constantly questioning life. We may wonder, "What will today bring? Will I have enough time? Will there be enough money?"

Psychiatrist Victor Frankl has said that it would be wiser to let *life* question *us.* When we look at the stars or a garden, for instance, life is asking, "Can you appreciate beauty?" When someone in pain comes into our lives, it asks, "Are you capable of sympathy?" At other times, life simply asks, "Do you ever allow yourself to enjoy?"

But the main question life asks, I believe, is, "What do you want from me?" And each of us has a different answer. Some of us want just to survive, while others want a lot of money. If you were asked what you want to do with your life, what would you say?

For myself, my vocation as a priest and a teacher might look like an answer, but there are many questions under the surface. Am I doing this because I have to or because I want to? Would I rather be in some other situation? Is there a deeply buried desire in me to be rich and famous even though I have taken a vow of poverty?

In trying to dig out really honest answers to these fundamental questions, I sometimes imagine what it might be like to be a celebrity or a cowboy or president of a large corporation. There is something attractive in many of these lifestyles, but I certainly wouldn't choose any of them for myself. More than anything else, I keep coming back to the fact that I do want to do God's work. I want my life to be an act of love.

The great psychiatrist Carl Jung said the specific crisis for those over thirty-five years of age is to find meaning in life. Before then, most of us are dreaming our dreams and carefully nourishing the seeds of hope; then reality sets in. We usually have achieved some of our dreams and have been disillusioned about others. More than at any previous time, we ask, "Does my life really mean anything?"

Jung also said he never treated a patient over thirty-five who did not have the basic need for a religious outlook. Being over thirty-five, I find that my faith does indeed help me sort out my preferences and clarify my values. I know I do not want to invest in anything that will sustain me only for a short part of my life.

I feel sorry, for instance, for people whose total identity is absorbed in being good-looking or having athletic talent because aging is inevitably going to change that. As you may remember, Marilyn Monroe, who was told that her whole value was in her face and body, killed herself on a Saturday night at age thirty-five.

Saint Augustine said that memory is a sad privilege when one has only days of delusion to remember. "Too late, O Lord, too late have I loved you."

When I was a young seminarian, I witnessed two bed-ridden old priests reacting to identical medical treatment from a brother in our infirmary. As the brother performed his services one of the priests was surly and complained, but the other was gentle and most grateful. I knew even then that someday I will be one of those two old priests— but which one? I guess it all depends on what I really want to do with my life. It depends on the answers I am giving to those simple questions that life is constantly asking me.

Am I the person I would really like to be? Am I doing with my life the things I would like to be doing? These are questions for the daylight hours. When the night comes, it will be too late.

Using Things, Not People

Imagine being a mother who has just polished the kitchen floor when your little child comes in with a handful of dandelions . . . and mud on his shoes which he tracks all over your newly polished floor. What's the first thing you say?

Or imagine yourself a father and your teen-aged son calls home to say that he had an accident with the family car. He admits that he rear-ended another car because he wasn't looking. O.K., Dad, what are your first words to him?

Situations like these ask us about our priorities. How important is a clean kitchen floor or an unblemished car? How important are the memories my child will carry through life? My reactions in cases like these say more about my values and priorities than I could say in any abstract self-evaluation.

For example, I could say to the first child: "Get out of here and take those stupid dandelions with you! You have just made a mess of my shiny floor." Or, "Thank you for the lovely gift, honey; let's put these flowers in water. And by the way, we have to remember to wipe our shoes before coming into the house, don't we?"

I could blast my son for the car wreck and recall all his other failures, or I could ask: "How are you? Was anyone hurt? We can always get another fender but we can't get another you."

Philosopher Martin Buber told of a time he was preparing a talk for a convention when he heard a knock on his office door. A young man with a troubled look asked if they could talk. Buber answered that he was writing an important paper and couldn't be bothered at the moment. The young man killed himself that night. A young life filled with potential was suddenly ended, and no one ever remembered Buber's paper.

On that night, life questioned him and Buber responded that his paper was more important than the person. He said that he will always feel the remorse of that decision.

We each have a limited amount of energy to spend on people and things. If there is one imperative in the Bible concerning this subject, I think it would be this: "Give your love to the persons in your life. Don't ever let a thing—whether it be money or pleasure or power—possess your heart."

One priest whom I knew very well confided his fears to me often, and his main fear was for the future. What would happen if our order did not get more vocations? "Where will we be?" he would ask. And his favorite line was "Who is going to push our wheelchairs?"

I recognized his insecurity—the same fears that lurk inside all of us. It is typical to wonder if I will always have enough time and money. It's easy to talk about using things and loving people, but who is going to push *my* wheelchair?

My priest friend died suddenly and at a rather young age. He never had to use a wheelchair!

Whenever we wonder if we are going to have enough, our Lord assures us: "Make your life an act of love, and I will take care of you. I will be with you all the days of your life. I will be your enough."

Now obviously a person must prudently try to provide for the future. At the same time, we are warned not to waste our energy fretting over stocks and bonds and who will push our wheelchairs.

I somehow feel sure that at the moment of our dying, we shall be glad if we have loved persons and used things. We will know that we have invested our talents well. Then we will be peaceful in the trust that Jesus the Lord will be our enough forever and ever.

The Christian Attitude
toward the World

We live in a world of many things and all of us accumulate certain "personal possessions," the mementos and trophies of our efforts, the objects of our enjoyment. It is important to inspect our attitudes toward these things, in order to avoid two somewhat opposite dangers.

(1) We can fail to use and enjoy the good things which God has given to us, or (2) we can be so enamored of these things that they own us: body, mind and spirit. These things can preoccupy us, make us so concerned about them that we gradually lose our freedom and capacity to love one another.

The first danger of temptation is a "world-rejection" mentality. Somehow this distortion has been quite successful in Christian history. Even though God so loved the world that he gave the world his only Son, many Christian teachers and preachers were fairly convinced that the only safe way to deal with things is to give them up. When I was a Jesuit Novice, we often began our sentences with "When I was in the world . . ." You see, we imagined that we were no longer in the world. I am not quite sure where we thought we were.

The worst venom of this world-rejection mentality in our Christian history was reserved for the human body, often referred to as "the ugly prison of the beautiful soul." The fact is, of course, that God does not make junk. According to Genesis 1, "God looked on everything he had made, and he was very pleased. He found it very good." And God calls us to join him in that pronouncement and appreciation: "It is very good!"

The second danger, at the other end of the spectrum, is the temptation to fall in love with these things of our world. The biblical command can be summarized: "Love persons, use things!" When we begin to love things, like money or power, we begin to use people to get these things. And so the Bible doesn't say that money is the root of all evil but "love of money." Jesus said, "Where your treasure is there your heart will be." Jesus encourages us to use and enjoy the good things the Father has given us, but he asks us to save our hearts for love and our love for God and for one another. When we love things, we use one another.

There is an old adage that we are all born with clenched fists but we all die with open hands. I think of the "clenched fists" as the symbolic expression of the good use and enjoyment of God's "very good" creation. Old Saint Irenaeus, in the second century, said that the "glory of God is a person who is fully alive!" The way we praise and glorify God is by using fully all the gifts and powers he has given to us: our senses, our emotions, our minds and hearts. This is what I call "the theology of possession."

But we all die with open hands. The open hands symbolize our freedom from possession by the goods and gifts of this world. We will not be owned or controlled by anything. The open hands hold up to God in offering all that I have or ever could have. "Take from me whatever could lead me away from you and those you have given me to love." This is the poverty or freedom of spirit which Jesus praised in his be-attitudes. This is the "theology of dispossession."

"O, Lord God," the clenched fists and open hands are saying, "I will use and enjoy all your good gifts: the sunrises and sunsets, the music and poetry of creation, the tastes and fragrances of each new day, the sights and sounds of the earth; but my heart has been saved for love, and my love will always be for you and for those you have given me to cherish. I will love persons, use things. I will be fully alive for your glory."

On Being "Poor in Spirit"

The Book of Genesis tells us that when God made the world, he looked upon his creation and found it "very good." It seems clear to me that God wants us to join him in this pronouncement: God's world is very good! But somehow our Christian history is marked with repeated attempts to run away from the world as a source of temptation.

This "escape" mentality is obviously immature. Running away from God's world to avoid temptation is a strange form of Christianity. To deny the goodness of God's gifts and his world reminds me of the poor man in the Gospel who buried his talents in the ground so he could feel safe.

If you were to make a list of your ten most treasured blessings, what would they be? To stimulate your thinking, I would like to share with you my own list of the gifts I treasure most and hope God will always allow me to keep:

● The gift of faith. Almost all the things I do derive their meaning from my belief in God and his loving presence in my life.

● Mental health. Losing contact with reality would seem to me like the end of a meaningful life.

- Physical health. When I feel good, I feel I can move mountains. On "sick" days, the mountains are on top of me.

- My membership in the Society of Jesus. Everyone needs a sense of belonging and this is where my roots are planted.

- My priesthood. If I could make only one statement to describe myself, it would be: "I am a priest."

- My special friends. With them, I can be totally open and yet feel totally safe.

- Music and humor. It would be hard for me to imagine life without music and laughter.

- A good reputation. More than anything else, I want to make my life an act of love, and it would be difficult for me to live with a general misunderstanding of my intentions.

- Success. I feel very sorry for those who really want to do good and meet only failure.

- Beauty. I could not imagine a world without beauty. The beauty of people, seasons, and stars is for me a reflection of the beauty of God.

I'm sure you have a similar list. Our real problem is to use and enjoy the good things of God's world without being controlled by them. I'm sure you can easily sense the difference between owning one's possessions and being owned by them.

In the Gospel of John, Jesus debates with his contemporaries. They insist they are "free persons, slaves of no one." Jesus tells them this is not so, because their tyrants are inside them: the worry over their possessions, the guilt for having used others for personal gain. He assures them: "If you accept me and my message, you will know the truth, and the truth will set you free."

The truth that sets us free is the truth that we are passing through this world on our way to God's house, where we will live with him forever. Jesus encourages us to use and enjoy the good things God has made, but never to give them the power to control or own us. How sad it would be if we became so fascinated with the good things of God that we forgot about the God of good things.

Jesus repeatedly warns us of this danger. He says it is harder for a rich man to get into God's kingdom than it is for a camel to get through the eye of a needle. He implies that it is difficult to have many possessions and not be seduced into some form of attachment. Such an attachment tends to obscure a sense of final destiny.

I have gone back over my list and asked: Do these items control me? If God asked me to give up one of them, would I be able to trust him? I have concluded that I am not completely free, but I am getting there slowly. Just asking these questions makes me reevaluate my attachments. My hands are gradually opening to God.

Always in the background is the realization that the day is getting nearer when I shall have to leave all these things behind. I hope death will not find me with my fists clenched around them. Perhaps it will be only in death that I will be free at last.

On Enjoying God's World

A line in the Talmud says: "Everyone shall be called by God to account for the legitimate pleasures which he or she failed to enjoy." Would you believe that many of us have only a diminished capacity for enjoyment? Some little demon haunts us, undermining our ability to let go and have a good time. We can eat a delicious dinner, attend a beautiful play, drive home on a lovely summer evening, and then go to bed unhappy because it cost $8.50 to park the car.

A possible explanation for this limitation of happiness is offered by Ernest Becker in his Pulitzer Prize-winning book, *The Denial of Death*. Becker contends that all of us have a deep fear of death because of our desire to be immortal. He also suggests we have a corresponding fear of life. We're afraid to take on reality, so we defend ourselves by reducing that reality to a small, workable size. We distrust our ability to cope with a larger world.

Most of us do this with pain and suffering. Whenever someone starts to cry, we instinctively say: "Don't cry." We're afraid to open ourselves to the vast tide of human suffering because we fear we will drown in it. But when we shut out the world's suffering, we also shut out its joy. We have only one set of doors to the world.

Some years ago, a psychiatrist came up with a system of group therapy called "Transactional Analysis." Dr. Eric Berne theorized that inside each of us is a *parent,* an *adult,* and a *child.* The *parent* is a collection of all the messages we received from our parents and other influences as children. Then there is in each of us the *adult,* which is our own mind and will. The third person in us is the *child.* The child is the whole collection of emotions that every one of us experiences. There is a sad child that feels picked on and cries a lot. But there is also the happy child who laughs and sings and jumps.

The key to our personal growth is to keep the adult in charge. The adult looks over the parent tapes, keeps some of the messages, and disputes others. Some of us allow our parent tapes to take charge of our lives. If one of the dominant recorded messages is: "This is a cold, cruel world," or "Life is a struggle," then we will feel lonely and mistreated. Our child will be sad.

But the adult in us can always intervene. The adult in us can record a new, optimistic message over the sad parent tapes: "Hey, this is God's world and it is very good. God wants me to be happy. Happiness comes from the inner realization that God loves me. He has made a beautiful world for me to live in, and wants me to enjoy the journey I will make through this world on my way home to his house. I will someday inherit all of God's estate, but part of my inheritance is God's presence in me right now. And he is also present in his beautiful world." What happens is that we gradually develop a "mindset." It is as though we set the dials of our minds to see all the beautiful things God has made. The adult in us urges the child in us to sing and dance and rejoice in the created goodness of God.

I suspect most of us fearfully expect the Lord to ask us about our failures on Judgment Day. Won't we be surprised when he asks us why we didn't enjoy life more? I think he will feel sorry for us when we have to account for all the legitimate pleasures we failed to enjoy. But at least the child in us will be able to sing and laugh for all eternity when we finally get to our Father's house and realize it is to be our home forever.

We Jesuits have a rule that we are to "seek and find God in all things." I once knew a man who knew he was dying a couple years before he actually left us. For those two years, he hid little surprises, made secret cassette tapes, and planted flowers that would come up only after he had gone. When all his secret mementos started surfacing, his family knew his purpose. His presence and love remained with them always. Similarly, God and his great love for us remain ever with us: in nature walks, picture albums, and geese in flight. In all things, God is waiting for us to seek and to find him.

The Christian Attitude
toward God

"No, I shall never believe in the God who condemns material things . . . the God who loves pain . . . the God who flashes a red light against human joys . . . the God who always demands 100 percent in examinations . . . the God who does not accept a seat at our human festivities . . . the God who does not have the generosity of the sun, which warms everything it touches.

"No, I shall never believe in such a God." This is a quotation from the book *The God I Don't Believe In*, by Father Juan Arias, a Spanish priest.

The Book of Genesis tells us that God created us in his image and likeness. I think that perhaps our most serious and prolonged heresy is that we invert the words of Genesis and make God in our human image and likeness. Saint John says that "God is love." This means that God does not *have* love but that he *is* love. Love is his very nature. All God does is love. All his actions in our world— from the first moment of creation—have been the actions of love.

Sadly and heretically we have persisted in making God like us instead of trying to be more like him. We have made him petty, outraged, fearsome, anything but loving. We have often presented the caricature of a small, pouting god instead of the portrait of a God who is love. As a result, I think, many of us have lost interest in God and drifted off into a humanistic type religion which makes psychology its savior and which worships at the altar of the sciences.

God is like the sun, which only shines, giving off warmth and light. In the same sense, God only loves. We can stand under the sun, stand in its light, and feel its warmth. But we can also leave the sun, blocking out its light and warmth, partially or completely. We can hide under a shade-umbrella or lock ourselves in a dark and cold dungeon, but—and this is what is important—the sun does not go out. The sun does not change because we leave it. In the same way, God is love, and we can open to his love or we can run from his love.

We can even lock ourselves in the dark and cold dungeons of serious sin, but—and this is what we can never forget—the sun of God's love does not go out. The only change that results from our sins is in us: We grow cold and our world turns dark. When the Bible refers to the "wrath" of God, the reference is to this sadness in us.

God's love is an unconditional gift. Theologians call it a "covenanted" love. In our general human experience and literature we think of the love of a mother for her child as the most enduring and unconditional love. But it is this God who is love who says to us: "If a mother were to forget the child of her womb, I would never forget you!"

You and I can't afford only to nod our heads to this truth. It has to get into our blood and into the marrow of our bones. We have to sit with this truth and soak it in: God is love. We have to pray to the Lord to send his Spirit into our hearts so we can shout joyfully: "Abba (Papa, Daddy)! Abba, Father!" This knowledge is a very special grace from God.

It's all there in the life and words of Jesus, whom Saint Paul calls "the visible image of our invisible God." Jesus is the Good Shepherd, lovingly searching out the lost. He is the Divine Physician who comes to us because we are sick.

To his contemporaries, Jesus was the teacher who wouldn't deal legalistically in cases, and who recognized the supremacy of love. Jesus scandalized the Pharisees, the Teachers of the Law, the Chief Priests and Elders of the People: everyone except the sinners and the children. Sinners and children believed in him. He loved them and led them from darkness into the light.

It's all there in the famous Parable of the Prodigal Son, which Jesus proposed as an answer to the question: "What does God think of a sinner?" In the end the father takes his son in his arms and keeps repeating: "You're home . . . you're home!" The wayward boy had at last come back to the arms where we all belong: the arms of love.

God Is Love

I am a teacher, and to explore my students' concept of God, I usually ask them three questions. I consider these the three most important questions one can ask about God: Does God get angry? Does God punish? And, if you or I were to try harder and become better Christians, would God love us more? My answer to each of these questions is an emphatic and much-prayed-over "no."

First, I am certain that God does not get angry. Why? Because God is changeless. And so whatever is in God, as the theologians say, is always in God. So if God were ever truly angry, he would forever and always be angry. In that case, we would have to say, "God is anger." We know that the Bible refers to the "wrath of God." But all the great Scripture scholars say that that is only a figure of speech, an anthropomorphism that projects a human quality into God. Actually, God's nature is to love. "God," as Saint John writes, "IS love."

Also, we know that our emotional reactions are not an automatic response to a given stimulus. For example, if a person is mean to me, I could react in any number of ways. I could be angry or hurt. I could feel guilty and ready to apologize. I might even feel sorry for the other person.

It all depends on me and on what is in me. If I get seriously upset by the actions of another, I have put my happiness in his hands. I have given that person power over me. Now I can't imagine a God who would react to our weakness by getting angry at us. He would be giving us power over himself, putting his happiness in our hands.

Peter once asked Jesus how often we should forgive those who have offended us. Peter suggests seven times, but Jesus replies that "seventy times seven" would be more like it. So I can't imagine a God who would set limits on his mercy. And Jesus tells us repeatedly that we must love everyone, especially those who have offended us. Now can you imagine a God who gets angry? No, the scholars are right. God is love, and all he ever does is love.

Now to the second question: Does God punish? Again, my answer is "no." When I explain this to my students, I simply ask them: "Suppose I teach this course very well and offer you all the help you need because I love you and really want you to do well. And suppose you choose not to cooperate. You don't write the required papers and you don't study. When I record that you have failed, do I fail you or have you failed? Am I punishing you or am I merely recording your performance?" My students always agree that I am only recording their performance. I assure them that if they perform poorly, I will feel only sadness. I will want to ask them, "Why? What happened?"

You will recall my favorite analogy. God is much like the sun. The sun only shines. We can stand under the sun, share its gifts of warmth and light, or we can leave it. We can even lock ourselves in the dungeons of darkness. But the sun does not go out because we have left it. In the same way, we can leave God, but he does not change.

He only loves. We are free to reject the warmth and light of his love. If we do, we grow dark and cold and can even fall into spiritual death. But we are always free, and even when we are languishing in the dark, we know we can always go back into the warm light of God's love.

Finally, our third question: Would God love me more if I tried harder and became a better Christian? I feel sure that God would reply, "I couldn't love you more. I have given you all my love. Like all real love, my love is a gift. You are free to accept or reject it. Even if a mother were to forget the child of her womb, I would never forget you."

So my three answers are all no. God does not become angry; the so-called "wrath of God" is only a figure of speech. God does not punish; he simply records our performances. And God could not love us more because he has already offered us all his love for us to accept or reject. I truly believe this is the way it was in the beginning, is now, and ever shall be. God is love.

Telling the Good News

We believe that the Scriptures are the Word of God. God speaks to us in the Gospels. Which five Gospel truths do you think he wants to emphasize?

I know this is a review of previous material. However, it is very important here if we are to read the Gospels as "good news." For myself, I think God is telling us who he is. I read it very clearly: God is love. It is his nature. That means God does not get angry. Scripture scholars assure us that the "wrath of God" mentioned in the Bible does not refer to anger in God. It is rather a figure of speech. When Jesus was asked how God feels about sinners, he told the Parable of the Prodigal Son. The father in the parable (God) never gets angry at his wayward son. Further, Jesus tells Peter that love never stops forgiving.

This truth that God is love means that God does not punish. My students grasp this easily. They know that if they fail my course, it is not I who fails them. I only sadly record their performance. Likewise, it is God's will and hope that we succeed. If we wander away from him, he will wait for us, like the father in the parable. It is possible, however, that we may leave God and never come back. We can fail in the course of life and love. And, in the end,

God will regretfully record our performance. He will allow us the choice we have made. He is not a vindictive God, but a loving God.

The next truth I would list is that God loves us as we are. This is the only kind of love that can help us. You and I don't want to be loved for what we have been or for what we could be. If others were to love us in this way, they would be loving only a memory or a dream. But God knows that our human condition is one of weakness. Saint Paul says Jesus' primary quality is his compassion: He understands our weaknesses and loves us anyway.

After God tells us that he is love and that he loves us as we are, he tells us in the Scriptures how to respond to his love. Jesus assures us that our chief response to him will be in loving one another. In fact, when Jesus describes Judgment Day, he says that whatever we have done to the least of his children will be taken as being done to himself. In effect, Jesus is telling us that we are all brothers and sisters and that God is our Father. We are related by some-thing much stronger than blood. We have a true share in the life of God. The Trinity of Father, Son, and Holy Spirit actually resides in each of us.

Another strong message of the Good News in the Bible is the reassurance that God's providence rules our lives. Jesus assures us that the same Father who takes care of the lilies of the field and the birds of the air cares even more for us. Of course, there will be times when God will challenge us to grow. There will be crises of faith, in which our old forms of faith will die so that newer, deeper ones may be born. In these moments of trial God asks us to trust him. All things will work out well if we can "let go and let God" have his way with us.

Finally, there is a profound and repeated reassurance in the Gospels that we are a people of destiny. God has prepared a special place for each of us in his house. One of the place markers at the eternal banquet table has your name on it. We must go through the frightening corridor of death to get there, but we are not just dust destined to return to dust. We are God's children, and he has promised to share his home with us if we accept the invitation of his grace. We will be with him in happiness forever. For me, these truths form an overview of faith and a summary of the Good News.

Recently someone did a survey of those who had been raised in faith but who had given it up. Many said they had given up their faith not because it was too hard to believe but because it was too good to believe. This is the greatest challenge for us: to believe. The extent to which the Gospel comes to us as Good News is the extent to which we are willing to take God and his Word seriously. To do this we have to find ever-deeper roots of faith and pray that the Lord of Life will give our roots rain. Either we will believe in God or we will believe there is no God. Both are judgments of faith. But if faith in a loving God is only a dream, then we would have to say that the opposite act of faith is a nightmare.

Vanquish Your Worries

One time I gave a lecture to a large group on Death and Dying. The theme of my talk, however, was that "Worry is a mild form of atheism."

"Death is the ultimate worry, isn't it?" I was saying. "But what do we *really* have to fear?" (P.S. It's really hard living with yourself after a good lecture like this.)

Don't you hate it when someone gives you that old bromide, "Now don't worry . . ." I know that I always want to respond: "If worry were a faucet, I would just turn it off. But I just don't seem to have that kind of control over my mind."

But in the Gospel of Saint Luke, Jesus says, "Don't worry about what to eat and drink. Don't worry at all. Your heavenly Father knows your needs. He will give you all you need from day to day if you will make the Kingdom of God your primary concern."

Ah! But listen carefully to the ending: ". . . if you will make the Kingdom of God your primary concern." Where your treasure is, there your heart will be.

To me, Jesus is telling us not to let our strength and enthusiasm trickle out on trivia. "Don't worry about what you're going to eat or wear. Don't worry about who likes you and who doesn't. I will be your enough. I will take care of all your concerns if you will direct all your energy to the Kingdom of God."

In psychology this is called "sublimation." Turn your mind to God's Kingdom and let all those minor worries die of neglect. Get up, roll up your sleeves, and help bring about God's Kingdom. "Then trust me," says Jesus. "I will take care of everything else."

What is this "Kingdom of God" that we are all called to? Scripture scholars agree that it is the central message in the teachings of Jesus. In the concrete, it is God holding out his arms to us, asking us to come together—to come to him as members of his family.

The invitation isn't extended to us as individuals. We are called to come to God together. The Kingdom has a horizontal and a vertical dimension. I cannot look up into the face of God and say, "I love you," unless I look out to you on the horizontal level and say: "My brother, my sister, I love you."

We remember the words of the poet Peguy. "We cannot go to God alone because he will certainly ask us an embarrassing question: 'Where are your brothers and your sisters? You didn't come alone, did you?' "

This is the Kingdom of God. On the part of God, it is an invitation to us to come to him in love, to be his family, to live with him forever. This is a matter of faith, and faith is never easy. God is saying to each of us: "I have always loved you and wanted you with me. From all eternity, I have known you and loved you. Yes, you have always been a part of my mind and my heart. I could have made a world without you, but then no world without you would have been complete for me. You don't have to change so I will love you. You have only to realize how much I love you. Then you *will* change."

Making the Kingdom my primary concern sublimates all my energies into an act of love. I can never again worry about having enough. Jesus is and will forever be my enough. I can only ask one question from now on: "What is the loving thing that I can do, be, or say that will bring the Kingdom a tiny bit closer?"

Finding the Kingdom of God

Biblical scholars agree the central doctrine in Jesus' teaching is the "Kingdom of God." The divisive problem is the timing of the Kingdom. In the Old Testament, the words "Kingdom of God" are not used more than once or twice, but there is the recurring theme that God reigns over his people. The more we seek and do God's will, the more complete is his reign. We are free and so must say a free "yes" to the invitations of God's love.

In the New Testament, the Kingdom of God is like a coin with two sides. On God's part the Kingdom is his invitation to come to him in love as his adopted family. The same Kingdom on our part is our acceptance of this invitation. When we pray in the Lord's Prayer, "Thy Kingdom come. Thy will be done," we are praying that our human family will go to God together in love.

On God's part, the invitation of the Kingdom is unconditional. But on our part there is something of a condition imposed on our acceptance. We must go together to God. We are not invited to come alone, but to come with one another. We can't say "yes" to love of God without first saying our "yes" of love to one another.

Now to the timing problem. The Gospels report three different answers Jesus gave about the timing of the Kingdom: It is already here; it is coming within a generation, and it will come at an unknown day and hour. All three answers are part of Jesus' description of the coming of the Kingdom.

In our culture, a man may invite a woman out on a date. It is a first invitation. After a while, he may ask her if she will wear his graduation ring or fraternity pin. This second invitation implies a greater opportunity for closeness. Then he may ask her to marry him: the ultimate invitation to human intimacy as man and wife. But notice she must say "yes" to these invitations.

God's invitations to the Kingdom of his love are something like this. When Jesus says the Kingdom is here, he means that the invitation of God to a relationship of mutual knowing and loving has already been extended in his very person. God has become like us so that we can know him. Already there are signs: the blind see, the deaf hear, devils are cast out, and the poor hear about God's love for them. The invitation to the Kingdom is here among us in the person and power of Jesus.

But there is to be another, even stronger, invitation: "Some of you who are standing here will in your lifetime see the Kingdom of God coming in great power." Jesus is referring to his death, resurrection, ascension to the Father and the outpouring of the Holy Spirit upon God's people. In effect, Jesus is saying: "Please don't mistake my death for tragedy. I am laying down my life for those I love. My blood will seal a new and eternal covenant with God. After I am dead, my Father will raise me up and I will ascend into heaven. There I will tell him about you, about how much I love you, and he will send you another helper, the Holy Spirit."

So the death, resurrection, and ascension of Jesus, together with the gift of the Spirit, is a second stage of the New Testament invitation—to belong to God in a new and eternal covenant. It is like a marriage. Those who accept this invitation will be in fact the Church or Bride of Christ.

Then there is a third and final invitation. When this will come, no one knows for it will be the end of time. "You will see the Son of Man coming on the clouds of the heavens, coming to claim forever in the eternal Kingdom of God those who have loved him." If we think of the Kingdom this way, then all three Gospel statements can be reconciled and accepted as genuine statements of Jesus. This has been the traditional, consistent Catholic position.

Our lives are a microcosm of God's Kingdom, a personal version of God's scriptural invitation to all of us. Daily he invites us into his intimacy. His invitations to closeness may come at any time and in a million ways. Each time God comes into our lives to invite us to a new closeness, it is a unique experience. These are the hours of God for which we must watch and pray.

The Dynamics of Change

Almost all of us have dreamed about the person we would like to be. I know I would like to make three changes in myself: to be more peaceful and less driven, more tolerant of human weakness—both in myself and in others—and to be more God-centered.

The surest way to believe in change is to experience it in yourself. Ideally, the process goes something like this.

To begin, have a goal and a model. You may remember Nathaniel Hawthorne's story about the Great Stone Face. A little boy sees the outlines of a strong, handsome face in the side of a mountain and he goes there often to admire that face. As he grows up, he slowly realizes that his own features become like those of the face in the mountain.

I think all change happens like this. We keep thinking about the person we would like to be and, in time, see not only that our ideal *can* happen but actually *has been* achieved.

It is also a great help to do what is called positive imagining. With the stage and background supplied by our imaginations, we see ourselves as the persons we would like to be. Just as the astronauts practice their space adventures in a simulator on earth, so we, too, can practice on the stage of our imaginations.

I see myself, for example, as a peaceful, tolerant, God-centered person. I picture what it would be like and eventually the picture becomes so engraved in my imagination that it is always there for me. This is my face in the mountain.

The next step then is to take charge of our lives and assume personal responsibility for all our actions and reactions.

A newspaper columnist and his friend once went to a newsstand to buy a paper. The man selling the papers was mean and surly but the writer's friend remained kind and courteous. As they were leaving, the writer's friend told him how the newsstand clerk was always so grouchy. "And are you always so nice to him?" the writer asked. "Yes, of course," the friend replied. "I don't want him to decide how I am going to act."

The writer devoted his next column to the incident, observing that one of the most important lessons in life is how to be an actor, not a reactor. I must decide how I am going to act, and not let others make those decisions for me. That is not to say that I should deny my emotions or try to silence them, but I won't be petty when someone else has chosen to be so. I will be the person that I want to be.

The final and most essential step is to seek the help of God.

I am not an alcoholic, but I have always marveled at the movement called Alcoholics Anonymous. One secret of A.A.'s success is its twelve Steps of Recovery, which have become the blueprint for many other similar organizations.

Directly or indirectly, eleven of the steps mention God and our relationship with him. One of those steps reads (in part): "Praying only for knowledge of His will for us and the power to carry out that will."

To me, this is a model statement of our need for the help of God in any process of change. God is something like an electrical outlet. If we plug into that outlet, there is power to light or heat the room. If we truly want to change, then we have to make this connection with God.

His power is waiting to supply the enlightenment and strength we need to become the persons we want to be. Through God's help, we can conceive ideals; we can see a face in the side of the mountain. We can become what we were created to be.

Our Mind Machines

Did you know that you have a tape recorder in your head—one that is more sophisticated than a computer? It's called your brain, and everything you have ever experienced is recorded there.

Some of the messages recorded in our memories affect us subconsciously—that is, we don't even realize it.

For example, maybe you heard something like this: "The important thing is security . . . always keep a little money for a rainy day." Or, "Be a big success . . . make us proud of you."

Of course, there are unfortunately some negative messages in our brains, too, like: "You will never amount to anything." Or, "You can't tell people how you really feel, so keep it to yourself."

When we were children, just discovering the world, we wondered at its complexity and about what was really important and unimportant. And we recorded all the answers.

As children, we all probably learned more by example than by words. If our parents talked a lot about money, for instance, the importance of money was recorded clearly in our heads. Or, if we saw our parents engaged in contests of manipulation, somehow it recorded in us that this is how you get what you want.

I know there are messages alive and active in me which seem to be the result of my family interaction. For example, we had angry arguments, but we always kissed and made up. I'm still surprised when some people think that an argument means the end of a relationship. It's not, according to my recorded message.

All these messages that we took in as children continue playing in us—shaping our attitudes and influencing our behavior.

The image we carry about ourselves is kind of a summary of all these messages. Our capacity to relate to others and our idea of what is important and unimportant in life—what we call our "value systems"—are also the result, at least in part, of the messages we have recorded.

Now for some good news. Just as with a tape recorder, we can record over these mental messages on our mind machines. For example, if I am saying to myself, "I'm a born loser," I can start a new thought pattern that will blot out that old message. I simply start saying to myself, "I am a winner." The more I repeat these new words, the more instinctual they become. And soon I habitually think of myself as a winner.

I'd like to suggest that you take some time and write down the five or ten most influential messages on your mental tape recorder.

Then decide which ones you would like to keep and which ones you would like to change.

For those that you'd like to change, formulate new messages that you would like to record over those you want deleted.

Keep these new thoughts positive. For example, don't say, "I am *not* a loser." Your mind won't take that in as well as the positive message, "I am a winner!"

I personally have a whole set of these thoughts I keep repeating all the time. I post them on my bookmarks, on signs on my mirror, on my bulletin boards.

My latest new recording reads: "My life will be an act of love." To my mind, like Robert Frost's less traveled road, it has made a world of difference.

Personal Responsibility

If there is one problem we all have, I would nominate: denial. We all deny—even to ourselves—certain facts and feelings with which we find it difficult to live.

One psychiatrist I know theorizes that 90 percent of our actions and reactions are governed by "unconscious material." If I resented my mother, for example, but could never acknowledge that resentment, I repress that feeling. Then, without knowing, I act it out, taking out my hidden resentment on other women who come into my life. As long as I keep the original resentment hidden or "denied," I never realize that I am displacing my anger on innocent people.

Freud, who discovered the unconscious level of the mind, said that the things we have hidden in denial are like wood held under water. These repressed realities tend to surface for recognition, unless we are determined to hide them forever.

One important cause of our "denial" tendency is our early programming. From the beginning we are encouraged to please others or to compete with them. When you and I came into this world, we had only questions and no answers. Someone else started filling in the answers to our questions, started "pulling our strings," so to speak.

Others instructed us about the price of being loved and admired. We learned we would be loved if only we fulfilled the conditions of those who said they loved us.

An important part of the solution is to become an "owner" and not a "blamer." We have to become personally responsible for all our actions and responses to life. In other words, we can't say things like, "You make me mad. . . . That really bothers me. . . . She really drives me crazy." No doubt you have seen this sign: "No one can make you feel anything unless you give that person permission."

Other places, things, and persons can only stimulate what is already inside us. They cannot cause things which are not in us already. So the profitable question is always: What is in me? One of the truisms about human nature is this: "Growth begins where blaming ends."

When Jesus enters our lives, he promises us that he is the Divine Physician seeking to help the sick. He assures us that he understands the human condition of weakness. He says the same "Shalom" (Be at peace!) to us that he once did to his fragile Apostles. He promises to love us into the fullness of life as he once did for those Apostles. His love is unconditional. It is important for us to know this.

I think that this is what Jesus means when he discusses human freedom with his contemporaries (see John, Chapter 8). He equivalently tells them that they won't be free until they believe in him and his understanding mercy. When they protest that they are no one's slaves, Jesus assures them that their tyrants are not outside, but inside them: the fears, the worries, the guilt they carry, the sense of inferiority, and the uneasiness they feel about the future. "Believe in me," Jesus challenges them, "then you will know the truth, and the truth will set you free."

Denial separates us from this reality. The hard fact is this: We are always accountable for our reactions and responses. No one else can accept this truth for us. But we can trust the Lord's mercy, reach out and embrace the truth of our fragility. The decision to accept ourselves as we are—in the human condition of weakness—will set us free.

Of Saints and Sinners

A well-known psychologist once compared our life goals to the rungs of a ladder. Each step represents the one thing that we want most in life. Someone living in grinding poverty, for example, is concerned only about finding enough food and shelter; when these are securely provided, that person can climb a step higher on the ladder and seek a new goal.

This thing that we want most—and it changes as we move along through life—gives direction to the whole course of our lives. And yet we are free always to change it.

In fact, in most lives there are such turning points which we call conversions. Saint Francis of Assisi, who grew up with fine laces and fancy things, for example, became the Little Poor Man of God. And Saint Ignatius Loyola, the proud soldier who sought power over others, hung up his sword in abject humility to become a companion of Jesus.

A humorist named Ed Wilock wrote a verse about all the great saints who had once been great sinners. It ends: "With God your was-ness doesn't matter if your is-ness really am." This is a humorous way of saying that what you *have been* doesn't really matter. It's what you are right now that really counts.

Saint Peter was another example of this kind of change. You will remember it was Peter who insisted that he would never deny Christ. And then he did just that. But according to the well-known *Quo Vadis* legend, Peter is leaving Rome in the year A.D. 67. Things are going very badly for the Christians. They are being crucified, thrown to the lions, and burned at the stake. Peter decides that "prudence is the better part of valor" and leaves the city.

On the Appian Way, Peter meets an apparition of Jesus. *"Quo Vadis, Domine?"* (Where are you going, Lord?) Jesus replies, "I'm going back into Rome, to die again and again with all the Christians who are giving up their lives there." So Peter goes with the Lord, back into Rome, to die.

There, on the Appian Way, at the place of the supposed meeting, stands a little chapel—the *Quo Vadis* chapel. In the sanctuary are two murals. On the right side is Christ on his cross. On the left is Peter on his cross. It has often been told that when Peter came to die, he was to be crucified. His last request was that he die with his head down. "I am not worthy to die with my head up. That is the way Jesus died." And so, on the mural, Peter is fastened to his cross—head down. The man who protested that Jesus did not want him, and who later denied on an oath that he even knew the Lord, had come a long way.

Sometimes I think that I come in two parts: part of me is loving, part of me is not. Part of me believes, part of me questions and doubts. Sometimes I feel like a pleasure seeker, at other times I am the power broker.

But as I get older I find myself believing more and more what the Lord tried so hard to tell his Apostles: If you make your lives acts of love, you will be very happy.

I find myself thinking back to the Last Supper and praying, "O Lord, empower my mind and energize my will to make all of my life an act of love."

Under all my zigs and zags and ups and downs, I somehow know that this is the only way I will ever be truly happy. Our hearts were made for love and they will not rest until they rest in love. Like Peter my values are sometimes a little shaky, but I think my heart is probably in the right place.

So now what are you doing with *your* life?

Developing a Conscience

The Christian understanding of conscience has always been this: a judgment of the mind about the morality of a given action or state. If I judge the local pie-baking contest, my conscience is not involved. But a judgment about returning money I find to its rightful owner involves morality, and whatever I decide will be a judgment of conscience.

Before age four, children have no active conscience. They know that if they break a window or hit their brother or sister, their parents will disapprove, but they really do not understand why these actions are wrong. Then, somewhere between three and five, children begin to understand rights and wrongs. They pass from external regulation of their conduct to an inner realization of right and wrong.

Needless to say, this step is not made all at once. In fact, some people never develop a true conscience. Some go through life respecting only external policemen. This is what is meant by an amoral person—one who wants to look good or stay out of trouble, but who has not really interiorized personal values.

At the other end of the spectrum is the "purely internal conscience." These people follow their own whims and want no one to interfere. "Don't confuse me with the facts. My mind is already made up."

Between these two extremes is the "true conscience," which is really an informed conscience. This person is like someone about to invest his or her life savings. Before we invest our money, we want all the information we can get. We study all forms of investments, stocks and bonds, and certificates of deposit. Only then do we make our own final decision.

In moral dilemmas we can turn to the Church. The Holy Spirit has been active for almost two thousand years in the minds and hearts of Christians. As one philosopher said, if we don't learn from mistakes of the past, we will repeat them. The voice of our Christian past speaks out of the wisdom of much experience.

The Bible, too, is the word and wisdom of God, distilled for us by prayerful believers. This divine wisdom has been carefully guarded through the centuries so that we can be enlightened. The Scriptures are not a catalog of easy answers for hard questions, but they do offer us a basic perspective from which good moral decisions can be made. To make moral decisions without consulting the Scriptures or the accumulated wisdom of two thousand years or without praying for God's enlightenment would be as ridiculous as investing our life savings without seeking knowledgeable financial advice.

In the end, we Christians must go alone into that little room of conscience. Sometimes the decision is not a torturous one. But circumstances often complicate many others. We know, for example, God wants us to honor our mothers and fathers. Still, exactly what we should do for our aged parents is a more difficult matter.

Our lives are shaped largely by our decisions. If we have made good decisions in the past, we find it easier in the present. What we are at the end of our lives will depend on how well we have interiorized true values and honored them with decisions of conscience.

And, of course, our moral decisions always have consequences. But the most serious consequence of all is what we ourselves become.

Making the Right Choices

A great psychiatrist, Karl Menninger, once wrote a book entitled *Whatever Became of Sin?* He thought we Christians had lost a sense of sin. He suggested that clergy were less than courageous in speaking openly about the reality of sin. Is this true? Do people still feel guilty or have we rationalized true guilt out of our vocabulary and existence?

First, we must ask: What is sin? One thing is clear: Sin must be the result of a free choice. There must be at least two alternatives, both offering advantages. Suppose I find your wallet with a sizeable amount of money in it. Your name and address are also there. My mind perceives that there are two choices and that there is a real advantage in each. I can return the wallet. This is the right and honest thing to do, and I will feel good if I do it. Or I can keep your wallet and money. It is not right, but it does offer advantages—think of all the things I could buy with your money.

I am now in the situation called temptation, standing between virtue and vice. The will, being free, can now direct the mind to focus on one of the two choices. If I choose to return the wallet, I carry out an act of virtue. But if my will directs my mind to play with the temptation, it will also challenge my mind to rationalize the wrong choice. No one ever chooses evil as evil. So I reflect that Robin Hood stole from the rich to give to the poor. I look at the money in your wallet and see you as rich. I, of course, am poor. Before long I rationalize that I am Robin Hood. Now I can keep your money and not feel guilty about it.

If I choose this immoral course of action, I may be troubled by a sensitive conscience. My mind may be unable to digest its own rationalization. So I have a second chance now to confess my failure or fortify my rationalization. If I choose the second, I will say things like: "You had it coming, leaving your wallet around," or "You would not have returned my wallet. Why should I return yours?" Eventually I will repress my guilt, driving it into my unconscious mind. But it will remain active even there. Human nature doesn't allow us to get away with sin. Perhaps I won't be able to sleep, but at least I won't know why.

Where there is actual sin, and we are all sinners, a sense of guilt is a healthy and hopeful reaction. It has been wisely said that "confession is good for the soul." It relieves me from the exhausting work of rationalization. When I admit, "I was wrong. I should not have said or done that. Please forgive me," I begin to experience the peace reserved for persons of good will.

But such honesty is rare. As children, we grew up blaming, projecting fault onto others. When God confronted Adam in the Garden after his sin, Adam said it was Eve's fault. Eve blamed everything on the snake. If we are not honest with ourselves, we will never be honest with anyone else. Our lives will become a charade.

Since we are all sinners, it is important to read the Gospels carefully and notice that Jesus is always kind and understanding to sinners. When Jesus first called him, Peter responded: "Don't come near me. I am not your type. I am a sinful man." Perhaps the closest friend of Jesus was Mary Magdalene, out of whom he cast seven devils. The Good Thief probably said only one prayer in his whole life. He saw the sign over Jesus' head indicating his crime: "This is Jesus of Nazareth. King of the Jews." The dying thief looked at Jesus with pleading eyes and asked: "I don't know where your Kingdom is, but would you remember me when you enter into it?" That poor man was promised: "This day you will be with me in Paradise."

It is important to recall the parable about God's attitude toward human sinfulness: the Parable of the Prodigal Son. We all need to imagine our loving Father running down the road to embrace us as we say: "I was wrong. I have come home." Our human fragility is a fact. But we must not let foolish choices separate us from our loving God, who understands and forgives our foolishness.

My Model of Faith

If I were to make a list of all the people who have influenced my life most, the person at the top would have to be my mother.

I think back to the days of my childhood when the sun streamed in the kitchen windows and everything in the house seemed secure because Mother was there. I'm happy I had the chance to thank her before she died, even though I'm pretty sure she did not understand the depth of her personal contributions to my life.

Someone has said that we do not seek a value and make it our own until we see it in someone else. And so it was with my mother and her faith in God. From the beginning, I remember her simple but bedrock faith. I remember the long prayers she used to whisper with fervor. God was the center of her world, her still point during all the storms of life.

Once near the end of her life, when she was badly crippled with arthritis, she crawled out of bed on the second floor of our family home and slowly and painfully negotiated the stairs. At the bottom, she later confided to me, "I remembered that I had forgotten my morning prayers." So I asked her, "Well, what did you do?" With a puzzled look she said, "I crawled back up the stairs, got out my prayer book and said my prayers." Her look seemed to be asking, Wasn't that what anyone would have done?

Another time when we thought Mother might be dying, I sat on the side of her bed and told her that a priest is a mediator. He shuffles back and forth across that bridge over troubled water, constantly bringing God to humans and humans to God.

I told her that I had just come across that bridge and I was bringing a message from God. "Mom," I said, "God wants me to tell you what a good and faithful person and mother you have been. I remember a lot of the beautiful things you did for us, the socks you darned, the Band-Aids you put on our bruises, the thousands of sandwiches you wrapped and put in brown bags for school. But there is so much that I do not remember.

"I am sure you said prayers in the middle of the dark night that I did not hear, and you cried tears that I never saw. But you know, the Lord remembers each and every one of the little kindnesses you did in his name."

I had a feeling that she was tolerating my long speech, but I do not think she thought that much about herself. When I finished, she reached up from her sick bed, took my head into her hands, and placed it tenderly on her shoulder—just as she did when we were little children. And she told me that the proudest thing in all her life was that God had wanted her little boy to be his priest.

Near the end of her life, my mother told me that death did not frighten her. But she added, "You know what I do fear, John? Pain." And then she looked up at the picture of Jesus at the foot of her bed in a way that only my mother could and she said with profound simplicity, "I asked him, 'When you come for me, Jesus, would you tiptoe in here and kiss me softly while I sleep?'"

About ten years ago, Mother lapsed into a coma. The doctor said that she would die quietly in her sleep. I looked up at the familiar picture of Jesus and said to him, "You are going to tiptoe in here and kiss her softly, aren't you? You couldn't refuse her anything."

My mother is dead now. But so much of what we are at any moment is determined by the memories we carry inside us. And for me, there are so many powerful, inspiring memories of my mother.

The Importance
of the Family

The family is the first and most important of all the influences that affect our lives.

When we come into this world, we are living questions. We ask: Who am I? Who are these other people? What is life about? The answers are conveyed to us in the hands that hold us and the voices that speak to us.

From the beginning of life, they also have been acted out in front of us and stored in us. We cannot recall many of these messages, but they are nevertheless active in us. In a sense, the hands that held us and the voices that spoke to us as infants still hold and speak to us. We tend to model our lives on these early lessons.

The family is the principal source of the first messages we record deep inside ourselves. Some messages are good and helpful, but others may be unhealthy and painful. Unless we learn to identify and edit them, we become prisoners of our recorded messages from the past.

The second source of family influence is based on a simple fact: *All experiences become memories.* Even the memories we cannot actively recall continue to influence us. Parents who take time to listen to or appreciate a child are not only offering a positive experience, they are creating a positive, lifelong memory. I am sure that much of what we are is determined by our memories.

Family *messages* and *memories* are vital and lasting influences, but there is a third "M" that also is transmitted by our families to us—meaning. The psychiatrist Viktor Frankl maintains that the quality of our lives is determined by the meaning we find in them. Finding meaning is a constant effort. If we are to grow, we must find new meaning in every new day. We must find meaning in joy and in sorrow, in education and recreation.

To find meaning in something means to find some value in it. If a person values only physical beauty, for example, life for him or her may be over at age thirty-five. We have to find a deeper meaning or we begin to die. We have to believe that there is a purpose in our lives. God sent each of us into the world with a definite message to deliver and a special act of love to bestow on others.

Psychiatrist Carl Jung believed only religious faith and love could supply this kind of meaning. And while faith and love are really God's gifts, God channels these graces through the faith and love of others—our families—who touch our lives.

Our parents are our first life models. If they were people of faith and love, the seeds of faith and love were planted in us. We took them on just as we took on other family traits. But if the messages, memories, and meaning in life are really family endowments, why do children of the same family often turn out so differently?

First, I suppose, because they heard different messages. It is not what we say, but what others hear that matters. And children are notoriously poor at interpreting their parents' messages. One child can hear love in the command to go to bed; another may conclude: "You don't want me around." It follows that if the messages are perceived differently, the experiences will be different.

It remains true that the script of our lives is written in our family relationships. Consequently, each of us must stop and reflect on the messages we are sending out.

We must investigate the memories that are shaping our lives and ask what memories we are creating in the lives of those we love. We must also ask whether we are really sharing with others the things that make life meaningful for us. Are faith and love the legacy we are leaving to those we love?

We must ask God to shape the messages our lives give to others, to let us be a positive experience and memory for them, and to deepen our faith and determination to make our lives acts of love.

We must investigate the messages, memories, and meaning that have been passed along to us, so that we may live fully and be a source of blessing to the lives we touch.

The Faith of Our Children

What will happen to the faith in the generations to follow ours? Will they hold the torch high or will the dream of a faith-filled world die?

There are, of course, no clear answers. We are all often wounded and broken, blinded by our prejudices and the values honored in our secular society. But something in me is certain that the God-given experience of faith is offered to all of us with great regularity.

We, of course, can help our children to keep deepening the discovery of otherness, to realize their own self-worth and the utter uniqueness of God. We can teach them to use language to express their unique inner reality. We can discourage them from hiding who they really are under the disguises of pretense. And we can teach them the value of an honest and informed conscience so they can think and choose for themselves.

All this is not easy, of course. I once said to a father of five how hard it must be for parents these days. "Yeah," he replied, "but it's even harder being a kid!" With that in mind, here are four things I would suggest to parents.

1. We should make sure that the religion we teach our children represents a happy and love-filled way of looking at things. We must drench their minds with the facts that they are uniquely created and loved by God.

"See others as your brothers and sisters, not competitors. Be tolerant with your own mistakes and those of others. Learn to laugh, especially at yourself. The only real mistake is the one from which we have learned nothing."

The teachings of Jesus provide many "rules for happiness." Never let things own you. Feel sorry for others who are suffering. Seek only the will of God, and we will be freed from many fears. Forgive others from their wrongdoings and we, too, will be freed from the damaging results of harboring a grudge.

2. It is impossible to find true happiness without an abiding sense of personal worth. We must affirm the young in all the honest and sincere ways we can. Without the lesson of self-worth, pretense will take over, and all other lessons will be wasted.

3. Another leg needed for a faith-filled journey through life is a sense of personal responsibility. I have found from my own experience that we must "own" our behavioral and emotional reactions before we can know ourselves and really grow.

4. And lastly, I have found that the young will listen to us to the extent that we listen to them. Honest and mutual sharing will call for the admission of one's own brokenness and fragility. To truly listen means to empathize. Simply put: "Tell me, what is it like to be you?"

Saint Augustine once wrote, "Man is man's way to God." And so we can help our young to become firm believers by helping them to be truly human. We have to love them enough to accept them however they are, and enough to motivate and inspire them to grow further.

We have to listen to and model for them. We have to love them enough to let them go through silly phases and faith crises.

So do let us pray for one another and especially for our young. And remember, the bottom line is, as always, "Jesus is the Lord of this world and human history." We must do our part and then in the end trustingly leave everything in his hands.

What Is the Church?

Once someone asked one thousand people to complete this sentence: "The Church is . . ." The first thing most of them said was: "The Church is . . . a building."

Of course, the Church has built many places of worship, so "building" is not a wrong answer. But at one time the Church had no special buildings. Strangely, this was when the Church experienced the greatest growth. What is the Church, then?

A seminarian explained the Church to his catechism class this way: He would announce that he was about to write the word "CHURCH" on the board. Then he would print, "CH . . CH." The children would remind him he had left out two letters right at the center: "U-R." "How true," he would say. "You are the heart and center of the Church."

This simple demonstration seems right on target. You and I, WE are the Church. We each have different graces and gifts, tasks and vocations. But together, we are the family of God. We are all baptized into the one Body of Christ.

A German theologian, Karl Rahner, defined the Church as God's "primordial or fundamental" sacrament. A sacrament is an external sign of God's presence—a kind of meeting place between God and us. Our Lord has promised us, "Where two or three are gathered in my name, I will be there."

In the Old Testament, God had made a covenant with the People of Israel. He would rule over and work through them as his special instruments in this world. Through them, God promised Abraham, "all the nations of the earth shall be blessed."

About five hundred years later, Moses sealed this covenant with God at the foot of Mount Sinai with a sacrifice and banquet, declaring, "It is now sealed in blood. We are the Chosen People of God."

Later the prophets of Israel insisted this covenant was only temporary and provisory. They foretold the coming of a Messiah and a new and eternal covenant. Many years later, Jesus went into the synagogue of his hometown, Nazareth, and told the worshipers: "This day their prophecy is fulfilled before your eyes. It is fulfilled in me."

The new and everlasting covenant of Jesus was offered not only to the People of Israel, but to all people. The new Chosen People of God would include all those baptized into the Body of Jesus.

Saint Paul calls this a "mystery," by which he meant a "plan." This, Paul says, was God's plan from all eternity, revealed by Jesus and to be realized now in us. Then Paul seems to reach deep into this mystery for its most profound implication: "Christ is in us." We, the Members of Christ, are the continuation of Jesus. We are the extension of Jesus to the ends of the earth.

It is something like this. In the mystery of the Incarnation, Jesus assumed a humanity to unify us and to invite us to share in the very life of God. Now God somehow assumes our humanities to continue his work of loving this world into life.

This assumption of our humanities is sometimes called a mystical incarnation and is accomplished by baptism. God claims us as his own. In baptism, we offer our hearts to God as his special dwelling place and our hands to continue his work.

This, then, is how I think Paul would have completed our sentence about the Church: "The Church is . . . Jesus living and loving in each one of us individually and in all of us together."

Paul would have assured us that we are never less than individuals because each of us is unique, and Jesus dwells in and works through each of us in a unique and highly personal way.

But Paul would also have insisted we are never only individuals because we are all united by an in-dwelling of God that is deeper and stronger than any other bond, even blood relationships.

We are united by Christ. For us, it is an assurance that we are never alone. Jesus is living in each of us, and in us he is loving this world into unity and the fullness of life. In Jesus, you are joined to me and I to you; you are my brother and sister, and I am your brother.

"CH . . . CH" can never spell the whole truth about the Church. You are and I am that Truth. We are his Church.

Finding the Path
to Christian Unity

Once, when I was keynoting a convention sponsored by a Protestant group, the convention leaders asked me to come into a private room, where they apologized for what they considered an embarrassing situation. A woman had driven up to the convention center and set up a sign reading: "John Powell is the devil. Catholic priests are all devils." I was not offended, but I was surprised at this passionate display of prejudice.

There also is a joke about Saint Peter leading a group of Protestants through the corridors of heaven, but urging them to keep silent as they passed a large room: "The Catholics are in there, and they think they're the only ones in heaven."

I suppose it offers some strange form of comfort to feel that we're on the winning team, that other people are wrong or inferior. The good guys just wouldn't stand out unless there were bad guys. Religious prejudice is especially sad because all Christians believe that the same Holy Spirit is guiding us. And, as you know, Jesus prayed to the Father that "all may be one as you are One with me and I with you." Saint Paul also spoke of One Body, One Spirit, One Lord. The same Paul, in his Letter to the Ephesians, asks us "with all humility and meekness, with patience, bear with one another in love, and be careful to preserve the unity of the Spirit and the bond of peace."

Of course, there are points of disagreement among Christians. We have to learn how to disagree but still love one another. However, the most important realization is that there are points of agreement. There are many things we share in common, and they far outnumber the differences. It is obviously more important to focus on them.

What are these common points in our Christian faith? Well, we share many of the things that go into building up the life of the Church. For example, we believe in the Word of God, the life of Grace, the virtues, prayer, and the gifts of the Holy Spirit. We have faith in the same Lord, Jesus, and we believe that God is our origin and destiny.

The Catholic Church, especially after Vatican II, has promoted dialogue among the Christian churches. The bishops at Vatican II said the ecumenical movement "embraces those activities and enterprises which, according to the various needs of the Church and opportune occasions, are started and organized for the fostering of unity among Christians." The Fathers of the Council insist that "through such dialogue, everyone gains a truer knowledge and more just appreciation of the teaching and religious life of both communions."

Is the eventual unity of all Christians a realistic hope? We all know that nothing is impossible for God. But this can happen only if we want Christian unity more than we want to be right. The point of our meeting is clear. We will meet in Christ Jesus. But it is only mutual love and mutual respect that will free us from prejudice and antagonism, and lead us to unity.

Am I saying that it really doesn't matter which Christian church a person belongs to? Of course not. I am a Roman

Catholic because I believe that the fullest contact with God is possible for me in the Catholic Church. I believe in the Catholic Mass and sacraments, and I believe in the teaching authority of the Catholic Church. But I also believe that the same Jesus and his Spirit are at work in other Christians and Christian churches. Thus the Vatican Council urges us Catholics to try to understand the outlook of our separated brothers and sisters, their religious psychology and cultural backgrounds. Understanding another is a real gift to both parties.

We are all pilgrims, walking toward our Father's house. We are taking different paths at the moment, but we are sustained by the hope that, if we truly love one another, our paths will meet and we will be joined in Christian unity. We will then be one in Jesus as he is One with the Father. Love can accomplish this. Prejudice can only delay it.

Forgiving Sets Us All Free

I have a friend who is willing to bet all his possessions on a theory. He contends that whenever a relationship breaks down, under all other things that are said and done there is always a lack of forgiveness.

At first, I thought this was a risky bet. Then I began to think about all my experiences, and just as my friend said, there at the bottom line of breakdowns was written, "I do not forgive you."

When Peter asked Jesus, "How far should we go in this matter of forgiveness . . . up to seven times?" Jesus tells him seventy times seven would be more like it. In other words, you just don't stop forgiving. Before there is forgiveness there are really two burdens: one person is carrying the burden of guilt and the other person is carrying the burden of resentment. Forgiveness sets both parties free.

My friend also told me about an ancient Hawaiian family ritual of forgiveness which was designed to restore and maintain a loving relationship among all the members of a family. This rite was conducted at least once a year but it could be held whenever there was a pressing problem.

The leader of the family would call everyone together and if an individual wanted to remain a member of that family, he or she came. The rite then began with a prayer that everyone would be honest and open with one another. The ancient Hawaiians felt that truthfulness and sincerity had to be the rocks on which everything else is built.

After the prayer the leader would begin the second part—an honest admission of all wrongdoings, grievances, and resentment. And if restitution was in order, it was made there and then or plans to have it done in the near future were made.

The third part of the rite then was forgiveness. And this was viewed by the Hawaiians as a release from all tensions in the family, all resentments, and obviously from all guilt. Then the leader of the family made it clear that the matter was finished and forgotten, never to be acted upon or brought up again. The person forgiven no longer had to bear the burden of guilt and the person doing the forgiving no longer bore the burden of resentment.

The Hawaiians knew they needed the help of God so the ritual ended with a prayer that love and peace would again prevail and characterize all their relationships.

Only with true forgiveness can we be released from all our tensions, grudges, resentments, and thoughts of vengeance. Going over my own failures somehow makes it much easier to forgive others. Some of the things I have done and some things I should have done but failed to do remain clouded in mystery for me. "Why did I ever do that? Why did I ever say that? Why didn't I keep my promise? How could I have been so blind?"

I am reminded that in our own self-knowledge we know only the tip of the iceberg. Under the waters of our lives are many unseen influences that so easily throw us off balance. Now if this is true of you and me, it's true of all others who need our forgiveness; they may not know why they did or said whatever it was.

I have often thought about little Saint Maria Goretti, who was stabbed to death when she refused to submit to an attacker. After serving a prison sentence this man became a brother in a religious order. He testified at her canonization process that as the dying girl was being taken to the hospital she kept repeating, "I forgive you, I forgive you." I suppose that's why saints experience so much of God's peace; they know that forgiveness is a part of the truth that sets us free.

Of Facts, Faith, and Love

The late Father John Courtney Murray once proposed that our country is venturing into an area where angels fear to tread. He foresaw that we not only could not agree on what is morally right and wrong, but that we did not even have an accepted basis for making moral decisions.

This is true even for our highest court, as former Supreme Court Justice Oliver Holmes described it: "Whatever the courts decide: this is what makes an action right or wrong."

And so, in 1857 the Supreme Court decided that Congress has no power to prohibit slavery and that the Missouri Compromise limiting slavery was unconstitutional. Then in 1973 the court declared in a similar decision that all state laws prohibiting abortions are unconstitutional. Since then, some twenty-five million lives have been ended because the court decided the unborn have no right to life.

The problem of our society is deeper than mere knowledge. I believe that the Supreme Court members knew when human life begins. Ten years before, an issue of *Life* magazine on human reproduction said clearly: "Human life begins at conception."

The deeper problem is this: knowledge does not produce virtue. *Knowing* what is right does not compel us to *do* what is right. What must be added to education, if it is to be effective, are faith and love. Knowledge, of course, is good and necessary. And we must be informed about all the biological facts of human life. But such knowledge is not of itself a motive. This is where faith and love must begin their gentle but forceful influence.

I would like to share one of my own experiences that has left me a changed person. A woman I have never seen once wrote me that she had been raped and had conceived a child by this rape. She wrote: "I am writing to you because you are the only one I know who would tell me to have this child. Everyone I know, including my own family, has urged me to have an abortion. But I have told them, 'The man who did this to me has done a terrible thing. But the baby has done nothing wrong. I just can't kill this baby.' "

So we corresponded for the length of her pregnancy. I told her what a hero she was to me. "I give the cause of life only words. You are putting your very life on the line."

So she delivered her baby. A photographer captured the first cry of that little face, and she sent a copy to me. On the back, she wrote: "This is the baby. Isn't she dear? Thanks for your love and support. They were very important to me. Without them, this baby might not be alive today. Love, [signed]"

This lady will always be a hero and a reminder to me. It is a terrifying thing to reflect that twenty-five million lives have been sacrificed. But knowledge alone will never guide us out of this dilemma. It must be accompanied by the warm compassion of faith and love.

A Time to Be Grateful

I believe that the secret of lasting peace and happiness is to be grateful always and for everything. Oh, it's natural to be grateful for the good things, for the successes. Palm Sunday is easy, but Good Friday is often very difficult.

How could one be grateful for tragedy or failure? Over the years, I have come to believe that God does indeed draw goodness out of seemingly bad things. God turns tragedy into beauty.

I have always had a compassionate feeling for Jeremiah the Prophet. When God called him to be a prophet, Jeremiah tried to decline. "I'm too young. I'm shy . . . and besides I have a speech defect." He has come to be known as the "reluctant prophet."

In the middle of his prophecy, he doubled up his fists until his knuckles were white. "You didn't make a prophet out of me," he sputtered. "You made a fool out of me. I'm not going to prophesy for you anymore. Oh, I'll probably go out and be your goat again, but I really don't want to!"

As a seminarian, I once wrote a term paper in the form of a letter to Jeremiah. I assured him that although things may have looked bleak during his lifetime, he has since become an inspiration to millions of us. I assured him that God can bring His own kind of success out of our seeming failures. The reluctant prophet has probably spent part of his eternity thanking God for that call and those failures.

As someone has said: "I don't know what the future holds, but I do know who holds the future."

I remember the widow of a Chicago policeman killed in the line of duty. He left her with nine children—the baby only six months old. One night in a prayer group, I was surprised to hear her say: "My husband's death was a real grace for me."

I knew of the tears she had shed, the sense of loss that lingered in her over the years. I knew about the letters she wrote to him after his death, attempting to keep up some kind of dialogue. But how a grace? How can one be grateful for tragedy?

I asked her afterwards if she could explain this for me. At the time of her husband's death, she explained, she was an overly reliant type. She depended on him for everything. Her own personality and personal growth had been somehow stifled and lost in his strength and determination.

When he died, she said, "I had to become my own person. I had to use all the strength that I had never called on before. I had to roll up my sleeves and work to raise nine children. Yes, for me his death was a grace. And for him, it was, I am sure, a better offer."

It seems that only trust can bridge the gap and help us be grateful for everything. Like Jeremiah, we have to believe that God will use our failures and turn our wounds into badges of honor.

Like the policeman's widow, we have to believe that the storms of our lives will turn into rainbows. We will someday see that grace has come to us through suffering, tragedy, and humiliation. For now, gratitude remains a matter of trust.

This month of Thanksgiving is perhaps the perfect time to reflect on being grateful for everything, even for the things we cannot now understand. In the beauties of autumn, we must prepare to be grateful for the long days of winter.

For all that has been, "Thank You!" For all that will be, "Yes!"

Two Essential Gifts of Love

Holidays always remind me of how other people are God's gifts—gifts of love to one another.

As gifts, we seek to say, to be, to do that which is best for the one who is loved. But sometimes, I admit, I don't know what is best for others who come into my life—people I'm trying to love. Should I be tough? Should I be tender? Should I speak up or shut up? I have to guess and ask God to bless my stumbling efforts.

There are two essential gifts of love, however, that I think we can't go wrong in offering each other. These gifts are always in order and always a part of the best for others.

I consider the first essential gift of love to be that of ourselves through self-disclosure. To tell each other who we really are. We are each as unique as our fingerprints. As the poet e. e. cummings wrote, "And now you are, and I am now, and we're a mystery which will never happen again." If you choose to withhold your gift from me, I will forever be deprived of sharing the unique mystery and experience that is you, for this is yours alone to give. And the same thing is true of my sharing myself with you.

Some time ago I was given an anonymous bit of writing called *Persons Are Gifts*. It described in wonderful terms just how we must accept each other unconditionally as gifts. People, the article said, come already wrapped— some beautifully and others less attractively. Some have been mishandled in the mail, others come special delivery. Some are loosely wrapped and easy to open, others are tightly enclosed. But the wrapping is not the gift. My gift is me and your gift is you. It's easy to make a mistake and judge the contents by the cover.

The second gift of love is to give the beloved an increased awareness of his or her unique goodness. In a sense, your interior image of yourself is in my hands and mine is in yours.

This is an especially important gift because a good self-image is essential to a happy life. If you don't like yourself, I can't imagine how you could ever be happy. You'll be spending every moment of your life with someone you don't really like. And if it's true we act out whatever we think we are, then you will develop obnoxious mannerisms to match your supposed unlikeable self.

It is also true that if anyone else tries to love you, you will suspect his or her motivation. You won't be able to imagine that someone else could possibly love you if you don't think of yourself as lovable.

On the other hand, if you truly do appreciate your unique goodness and giftedness and you see these as God's gifts to you, I don't know what could make you unhappy. You will be living with someone you truly like twenty-four hours a day. When you act out your self-image, you will be pleasant and peaceful because you are content within yourself. And when others express their love for you, you will be able to take it in, to believe in it and to treasure the gifts of love that have been offered to you.

This second gift is the feedback of what is called affirmation. By your eyes, words, smiles, and kindnesses to me you will remind me that I am a uniquely good and gifted creation of God, and I will try to do the same for you.

And the God who has made us in his image and likeness will smile upon us. The Lord who has asked us to love one another will whisper into our hearts, "Well done, my good and faithful servants. Whatever you do to the least of my children, I will take as being done to myself."

Signs of God's Love

Some years ago I was counseling a young woman who—I admit—shocked and educated me. She told me that she was three months pregnant. Then she looked at her shoes and whispered: "But I have an appointment next Thursday to kill this baby."

I immediately told her all the reasons to keep her baby. "If you need money or a place to stay, I'll beg it for you. If you give your baby a chance at life, be assured that I'm with you all the way. But, if you end your baby's life, of course . . ."

Then came the moment of my education. With eyes brimming with tears, she looked up and said: "I know you love my baby, but do you also love *me?*"

What does this have to do with Christmas? From my reflections on that day came the inspiration that personally changed my life: Unless we know that we are loved, we have little capacity to love anyone. That young woman in my office needed to know that someone loved her before she had any love to give to her unborn baby. Maybe what we all most need to know—more than any other knowledge—is that God loves each of us. "I know you are loving, God, but do you really love me?"

Saint John assures us that we can love only because God has first loved us (1 John 4:19). We have to drench our minds in this truth, and absorb it into every muscle, fiber, and brain cell. To the extent that we grasp this, we will be energized to love God and others. That will indeed be Christmas for us. Then maybe for the first time, the world will make sense and life will have meaning.

The 139th Psalm thanks God for watching over our lives. "Wherever I am, you are there, watching over me, taking care of me. Even in the darkness of night your light surrounds me." The psalmist goes on to thank God, "For you created my inmost being: you knit me together in my mother's womb. I praise you because I am wonderfully made. Your works are wonderful. Oh, I know that!"

The signs of God's love are all around us, but only the eyes of faith find them. I remember a story about some children playing "Hide-and-Seek." One little boy hides himself very well but after a while discovers that no one is looking for him. I often think that God would like to tell us how often he is in that position. "The signs of my love are all around you. But are you looking for me?"

In giving us his Son in human form, God was speaking our human language. He was telling us in a way we can understand that he loves us. "I love you. In fact, I have loved you with an eternal love. That's why I chose you: to share my love with you. I have even carved your name on the palms of my hands so I won't forget you. Even if a mother should forget the child of her womb, I would never forget you. I have sent my Son into the world to tell you all this."

Saint John also tells us that God is love (1 John 4:7). God's nature is to love; all God ever does is love. We are free to leave God, which we do when we sin, just as the Prodigal Son wandered from his home. Nothing can separate us from God's love except ourselves and our own free choices.

I would say that the heart and soul of a personal Christmas is just this: God so loved each of us that he gave his only begotten Son so that we might have eternal life—both now and forever—so that we in turn might love ourselves, God, and those others who are around us.

God's Plan for the Nativity

I sometimes imagine God has put me in charge of planning the Nativity of his Son.

In my imaginings, I command unlimited resources, so I feel obliged to plan a real extravaganza. I get an office with a bank of telephones and a competent staff. I make it clear to my staff that this will be the most important event in history. Nothing can go wrong.

First, we go over medical arrangements. I order a new hospital with the latest equipment and the best obstetricians and nurses. Then I tell my staff to arrange modern transportation to take Mary and Joseph the ninety miles from Nazareth to Bethlehem—maybe a long, sleek car with a padded interior. And hire a chauffeur who knows the way. If we get the Holy Family lost, we will be the laughing stock of posterity.

Since Jesus is to be the Savior of all, the whole civilized world should be informed. We contact the best public relations firm to plan a media blitz for early December. Invitations go out to every ruler. I want to see the road to Bethlehem filled with dignitaries on their knees in adoration. It will be a good example to the rest of the world.

When Jesus is born, fireworks must light up the skies. One star over Bethlehem will never do. And we need someone—Johannes Brahms, perhaps—to write a special lullaby. When the Mother and Child are up to it, we can start the adoration line. Gold is an acceptable gift, but frankincense and myrrh are a bit tacky. . . .

Then I laugh at myself and remember God telling us: "My thoughts are not your thoughts. My ways are not your ways." Because Caesar Augustus wanted a census, Mary and Joseph had to make the four-day journey to Bethlehem. Perhaps Mary rode part of the way on a tired donkey, but the roads were crowded and they had to sleep in the fields. Their reception in Bethlehem turned out to be a sad rejection: "No room in the inn." So Joseph had to take his wife to a cave used by shepherds to shelter their flocks. There the Son of God was born. The first people to see the Word made flesh were simple shepherds, the lowest caste in a class-conscious society. By making them first, God proclaimed that there are no more outcasts: "The least of my children are very special to me." The shepherds stood outside the cave and asked Joseph if a boy had been born there. "I know it is hard to believe, but an angel directed us here. The angel told us not to be afraid."

Joseph replied: "God's messages always begin that way. He said that to my wife when he asked her to become his Mother. He said that to me when I was struggling to understand all this. Come in and see the Child, and do not be afraid."

When the shepherds leave the cave—their faces glowing—I am there to meet them. I tell them how I would have planned all this. They stare sadly at me. They cannot understand. The simple often know what is important and unimportant.

Joseph leads me to the Mother and Child. Two things strike me immediately: the smallness and helplessness of the baby who is really God and the peace on his Mother's face. I must remind myself that the hands that shaped the mountains and flung the stars across the skies have become small and helpless so I will not have to be afraid. The voice that commanded this world into being has become weak so I will not have to be afraid.

Later this voice would tell all who would listen that the only way to true happiness is to be "poor in spirit." Don't let things possess your heart so that there is no room in the inn for the poor and the shepherds. He would tell us true peace is discovered only by the "pure of heart." Make love the only motive in your life and you will be truly happy. Then I recall the peace on his Mother's face, and I understand the effects of being "poor in spirit" and "pure of heart."

I cannot tell Jesus of my plans for the Nativity. Had I been in charge, his whole message would have been lost. Christmas helps me realize what is important and unimportant. I suppose that is why God, whose thoughts and ways are not mine, chose to be born in a cave in Bethlehem.

Peace on Earth

Spiritual writers have long maintained that inner peace is a sure sign of God's presence. But what is "inner peace"?

One meaning, I suppose, is a profound sense that all is well. Jesus said that this inner peace would be his lasting gift to us: ". . . a peace that the world cannot give . . . a peace that the human mind will never really understand."

Of course, Jesus does not promise us a problemless life. However, the peaceful person experiences a certain security in dealing with the problems of life. As someone once said, "I don't know what the future holds, but I do know who holds the future."

Sometimes it is easier to recognize inner peace in others. One author wrote how this peace was a distinguishing mark of the Mother of Jesus. Just listen to the Magnificat. While carrying Jesus in her womb, Mary exclaims to her cousin Elizabeth: "My soul magnifies [makes much of] the Lord. My heart is glad because of God my Savior. For God has smiled down upon me, a little servant girl."

I have often thought that Mary's peace grew out of her knowledge that God had smiled on her and blessed her. She made much of God's goodness. I suppose that anyone who reflects on it knows that God has blessed every one of us with unique gifts.

I once knew an elderly woman who seemed also to personify this peace. She didn't really place much value on material things. She made much of the Lord and of loving others.

I think that Jesus would surely have called her "pure of heart." She was, however, a source of embarrassment to her children; she insisted on wearing an old winter coat that had seen better days. So her frustrated children finally took up a collection among themselves and bought her a new coat. And Mama seemed to be very grateful. She was always good at being grateful.

Later, when the family was going out for dinner, though, Mama put on her old cloth coat. The children tactfully suggested that they would like to see her in her new coat. Without a moment's hesitation, the mother confessed, "Oh, I gave it away."

It seems a poor woman had come to the door and asked for some food. "But the poor dear had on an old coat with holes in it, so I gave her my coat so she could stay warm." The amazed children asked Mama the obvious question: "Why didn't you give the lady your *old* coat?" Mama looked puzzled for a moment; then she asked: "We're supposed to give others our best, aren't we? Isn't that what Jesus said?" It's hard to argue with that kind of goodness.

Sooner or later we must ask ourselves: "What do I make much of?" The right answer to this question, I believe, can put our feet on the path to peace. What do I think about most often? What demands my attention? And what worries me?

We may have to sit with these probing questions for a long time, but all the answers are buried somewhere deep inside us.

The leftover leisure of the Christmas holidays is a good time to do this soul-searching. It is a good time to make a list of our personal blessings, a grateful count of all the gifts God has given us.

Maybe then with Mary we can share the realization that he who is mighty has done great things in us. We may discover that most of our struggling is from making too much of the wrong things.

For all your gifts and especially for the gift of your Son who lives within us, thank you, Abba-God.